Capitalism, Primitive and Modern

BY THE SAME AUTHOR

Economic Development and Social Change in South India
Manchester, Manchester University Press, 1962

Capitalism, Primitive and Modern

Some Aspects of Tolai Economic Growth

T. SCARLETT EPSTEIN

Routledge
Taylor & Francis Group
LONDON AND NEW YORK

First published 1968 by Michigan State University Press

2 Park Square, Milton Park, Abingdon, Oxfordshire OX14 4RN
52 Vanderbilt Avenue, New York, NY 10017

Routledge is an imprint of the Taylor & Francis Group, an informa business

First issued in paperback 2019

ISBN 13: 978-0-87855-397-6 (hbk)
ISBN 13: 978-1-138-50789-0 (pbk)

To Bill, Micky, and Debbie

Foreword

A foreword to this book is gilding the lily. Scarlett Epstein is well known already for her excellent study of economic development and social change in South India, praised from the economic point of view by Sir Arthur Lewis. She has also published many articles on her research in India and among the Tolai of New Britain, including two in collections of essays on economic anthropology with which I have been concerned. This foreword then is a salute to a colleague as much as a continued declaration of faith in the importance of her contribution to a still too little studied subject.

I have no specialist knowledge of the Tolai area, but I visited Rabaul and its neighbourhood in 1951 for a brief space and was impressed by the vigour of the economic processes of the Tolai people, their lively political interests and their wish for independence of government control. I noted the wide range of cash transactions into which the people entered and the relative wealth and sophistication of their technical equipment. But I was struck also by the intermingling of traditional and modern elements in their culture: a house with a mixture of thatch, wood, and corrugated iron; an outrigger canoe side by side with a copra drier. I was astonished by the Rabaul market with from two to four thousand people at various times buying and selling an imposing diversity of local products: coconuts, canarium almonds, areca nuts, lime and betel leaf, peanuts, sweet potatoes, tomatoes, cucumbers, lettuce, melons, pumpkins, papaya, spinach, sugar cane, yams, maize, limes, aubergines, fowls' eggs, baskets, whisks. Most of the sellers were women coming in trucks and jeeps or walking in with head and back loads. What was of special interest was the fact that three kinds of currency were in use, shillings, cowrie shell strings, and tobacco. All the transactions I saw were in fairly small amounts, one shilling, one span string of cowries, one stick of tobacco, and it appeared surprisingly that there was no haggling. I was told indeed that all transactions were in quantities of a shilling, its multiples and equivalents, and that the size of the package given in return varied according to the state of the market.

In discussion with some senior Tolai people I heard what to an anthropologist even in those days was a startling suggestion —that their community should change their structure from matrilineal to patrilineal. According to my particular informant it was not fair that a child should not inherit from his father and that another man's child should. He argued that there was much support for the change. 'All like rausim this fella fasin' (people would like to throw out this idea).

I was not in the area long enough to check my observations, to find out how representative were the market practices, the level of economic achievement, the sophisticated, dynamic attitude towards the social structure. But I came away feeling the fascination of the social scene and the need for proper anthropological analysis of its components.

In this book Scarlett Epstein has richly set out for us the Tolai economic situation. With a wealth of carefully recorded detail and a stimulating theoretical approach she has examined the development of these people from a traditional shell money accumulating economy to a modern cash economy with achievement of a high productive order. The Tolai are remarkable for their rapid, massive response to the new opportunities presented to them by introduced technology and communication facilities. Dr Epstein has been able to explain how the flexibility of their social system and their partially monetised, traditional economy have assisted in these developments. Yet they have not abandoned all their former way of life. The limited labour requirements of their crops allow them to blend innovation with traditional institutions, and side by side with a lively interest in modern cash benefits they still accumulate cowrie shell strings for use in traditional transactions. Moreover, considerable as is their economic achievement in modern conditions, growing pressure of land, maintenance of traditional forms of land tenure, and lack of investment in commerce and manufacturing industry have tended to hamper their attainment of levels of capitalised enterprise comparable with those of the most developed sectors in the economy. Dr Epstein reveals with great skill the complex interrelationships involved in this whole situation.

The book is thus a contribution to economic anthropology in two major ways. It provides a most interesting example of the subtle interrelationships between traditional and modern forces in an economic and social system. It also faces frontally the problem of economic growth in a Western Pacific society, and by careful analysis demonstrates the significance of social factors for an understanding of economic problems.

London, November 1967

Raymond Firth

Acknowledgments

This book is based on field work which I carried out on the Gazelle Peninsula during fifteen months between 1959 and 1961 as a Research Fellow in the Department of Pacific Economics, Australian National University. The writing up of the material in this form was made possible by the award in 1966 of a Visiting Fellowship in the Research School of Pacific Studies, Australian National University. My thanks are due to Professor J. G. Crawford for his continuous encouragement in my work.

I am deeply indebted to many officers of the New Guinea administration for their help in making records available to me and the readiness with which they gave me the benefit of their own experience in the Territory, as well as for their warmth and hospitality. In particular I would like to thank J. R. Foldi, D.C., Rabaul; H. West, D.O., Rabaul; J. Emanuel, A.D.O., Rabaul; C. Liddle, A.D.O., Local Government, Vunadadir and their families; J. Lamrock and R. Pulsford of the Department of Agriculture; and K. Gorrenge and G. Dunn of the Tolai Cocoa Project.

My debt is greatest to my many Tolai friends and informants who patiently helped me to learn their language, put up with my many tedious and detailed inquiries and altogether spared no effort to help me understand their way of life. The Rapitoks not only generously allowed me to observe all their social activities, they also insisted that I participate in them, including taking my place as a member of the dance team at a large mortuary rite. To Bilak and his wife Ia Varpiam, in whose hamlet my house was built, were my constant guides and companions, so were many other Rapitok men, women, and children of whom I can mention only a few: Tarai, To Dungen, To Nelson, To Riet, Turme, Iaure, Ia Ngaime, Ia Delila. My local research assistants, To Peril, To Enos and To Magugu were tireless in helping me collect the data I wanted. I shall always gratefully remember the sincere friendship and hospitality the Rapitok people offered me; the coil of their most precious shell money, which they helped me to accumulate, serves as a permanent reminder of my stay among them.

My thanks are due to Mr E. K. Fisk who worked painstakingly through the manuscript and also to Professor J. A. Barnes for his comments on earlier drafts. I am also grateful to Dr H. C. Brookfield, who advised on the technical aspects of the topography of the Gazelle Peninsula, as well as to Mr H. Gunther for his assistance in drawing the maps.

Chapters 3, 4, and 7 first appeared in the journals *Economic Development and Cultural Change*, *Economic Record*, and *Australian Journal of Agricultural Economics* respectively. They are reproduced here in an altered form with permission.

Finally, I wish to thank my husband and our two little daughters who, throughout the period of writing this book, have borne patiently my ill temper and shortcomings as a wife and mother.

Canberra, September 1967

T. Scarlett Epstein

Contents

Tables

Plates

Maps

Introduction

This book is about the Tolai, a Melanesian people living on the Gazelle Peninsula of New Britain, to the north-east of the mainland of New Guinea. The Tolai are reported to have been cannibals until about the end of the last century (Pfeil, 1899:131), yet nowadays they are regarded as one of the most sophisticated and advanced people of the whole of the Territory of Papua and New Guinea.

I made a study of the Tolai in the years 1959-61, including two periods, totalling 15 months, living with them in a parish. This study revealed many particularly interesting aspects in the economic life and development of these people, some of which have an interest and significance which goes far beyond the affairs of the Tolai people and those immediately concerned with them. The purpose of this book is to describe and discuss these aspects of Tolai economic development and to analyse the general theoretical implications which emerge.

Economic expansion has become a problem of world-wide dimensions. Administrators and entrepreneurs in advanced economies are nowadays highly change-conscious; national income statistics are carefully collected and compiled with a view to examining the growth rate of economies. Growth rate targets are set and national policies geared to their achievement. Yet it must be borne in mind that economic progress is a fairly recent phenomenon even in what are now highly industrialised societies.

> From the earliest times of which we have record—back say two thousand years before Christ—down to the beginning of the eighteenth century, there was no very great change in the standard of life in the civilised centres of the earth. Ups and downs certainly. Visitations of plague, famine and war. Golden intervals. But no progressive violent change (Keynes, 1933:360).

The rapid and essentially continuous rise in per capita income in Europe and North America during the past two-and-a-half centuries, which has come to be regarded as 'normal' in these countries, is in fact a unique phenomenon in the history of mankind.

This recent and very rapid economic expansion in certain parts of the world has created a glaring discrepancy between advanced and underdeveloped economies: the former are wealthy and grow richer year by year, while the latter are poor and are only slowly emerging from their past economic stagnation. Most of these backward countries are former colonies in Africa and Asia. In many of these areas the rate of political development exceeded that of economic growth: political aspirations by far outstripped economic resources. Nationalist movements in these dependent countries made it clear to colonial powers that they had to be granted political independence. However, newly emerging states in Africa and Asia frequently found that, although they had gained political independence, they did not yet form economically viable units. Western countries realised the need to give financial assistance and other help to these newly emerging nations in order to ensure their survival and the persistence of democratic institutions. Western economists and technical experts were sent to draw up plans of development for these backward countries. But in a democratic system, which is the ultimate aim, the population cannot be forced to react positively to new economic opportunities.

The take-off into economic expansion in the advanced countries is well documented. By contrast, little is as yet known about the process of initiating growth in the underdeveloped areas of Melanesia and parts of Africa, many of which are still composed of a great number of small and fairly independent tribal or village economies. Frequently, environmental factors are responsible for this fragmentation and isolation, as, for instance, is the case in the Highlands of New Guinea. The rate of development varies considerably from society to society, depending on a combination of indigenous and exogenous social, cultural, political, and economic variables. Some of the major political and social variables are political institutions and organisations, and social mobility and flexibility in the traditional system of social relationships. Specialisation and trade, the internal economic potential, that is the proportion of unused resources (Fisk, 1962:466), market forces and other external influences (Fisk, 1964:158) are some of the economic determinants of growth.

It appears impossible to reduce the complex and intricate interconnection of all these different kinds of variables to a simple causal relationship with economic development. However, with small-scale societies such as the Tolai of New Britain, who were contacted by Europeans only towards the end of the last century, it is at least possible to attribute the beginning of economic development to the economic factors of the introduction of steel tools and the widening of the market with its different aspects—the availability of new and exotic consumption goods, the introduction of foreign currency, and so on. Not all so recently contacted societies have advanced at the same rapid rate as the Tolai. In some, the slow rate of economic growth has been a disappointment to planners and administrators, while in others the speed of change has been startling. Any observer of the Tolai cannot help but be struck by their quick and positive response to new economic opportunities.

At the end of the nineteenth century the Tolai were technologically still extremely primitive: they used sharp pieces of bamboo, stone axes, and pointed sticks as their main tools (Kleintitschen, 1906:16). Yet only fifty years later they already owned a large number of motor vehicles, as well as costly copra driers and cocoa fermentaries. In terms of per capita cash income the Tolai are still underdeveloped and poor. In 1959 their estimated per capita cash receipts, subsistence production excluded, amounted to no more than £25,* which represented only 11 per cent of the U.K. per capita income for the same year. Nevertheless, the Tolai of the Gazelle Peninsula already gave an impression of great wealth as compared with other small New Guinea societies.

*Monetary figures are given in £ Australian, the currency ruling at the time of my study. Prior to 1933 the £ Australian was at par with the £ Stg. Since then it equals only 16s. Stg. Australia changed over to decimal currency at the beginning of 1966.

In this book I try to examine the forces which facilitated this comparatively rapid economic progress of the Tolai and the obstacles which had prevented an even greater expansion as well as those which are likely to impede the path to future continuous economic growth. I attempt to analyse the impact of economic change on the traditional Tolai social system: what aspects persisted and what aspects changed. In Chapter 1 I provide some background information on the Tolai, their area and history of contact. In Chapter 2 I begin by examining in detail the traditional Tolai social and economic organisation as it existed before European contact. The flexible social system, operating with a monetised economy, provided a fertile ground for economic development. In fact, it can be regarded as having been a system of 'primitive capitalism', with great emphasis on thriftiness and accumulation of wealth rather than 'primitive communism' without any concept of private property.

In Chapter 3 I discuss the impact of European contact on Tolai economic life. This contact meant a widening of the market—foreign traders were keen to acquire coconuts and labour—and the innovation of new capital as well as consumer goods. By 1960 the Tolai had passed through four distinct phases in their economic progress. In the 'transition period' they got the first glimpse of the new tools and goods made available by traders either in exchange for Tolai coconuts or labour or both. During the second phase, the 'agricultural investment period', they rapidly extended their coconut plantings. They also increased their production of food crops to supply foreign settlers as well as the growing non-Tolai native labour force on the expatriate plantations in the area. This increase in production resulted in a considerable addition to Tolai income. However, since their consumption did not increase in proportion to their income, they began to look around for profitable investment opportunities for their accumulated cash resources. Consequently they entered their 'investment trial period' during which they experimented with enterprises in the sphere of agricultural processing, such as copra driers, and servicing industries, such as transport and retail trade. As a result of their inexperience of organising and operating enterprises, a high proportion of their initial ventures failed. However, they learnt by experience and, after World War II, passed into the fourth phase of economic progress, the 'tertiary investment period', during which the number of Tolai who owned vehicles and retail stores grew considerably and the proportion of business failures was greatly reduced. However, even at this stage agriculture still provided the basis to the economy.

In order to examine the process of economic change in a small-scale society I focus a microscope, so to speak, on one particular Tolai parish,* Rapitok, a frontier settlement, and discuss in detail the mutual interaction between traditional social organisation and the new forces of change. I lived in Rapitok for over a year and surveyed in detail most aspects of social and economic life. In Chapters 4 and 5 I discuss the way the Rapitok population interacted with the wider economy; the important part administrative policy played in shaping their economic progress, in that they followed the advice from the administration given since the last war and planted cocoa extensively; the development and profitability of transport and retail enterprises. Economic differentiation in Rapitok was expressed in terms of productive rather than non-productive assets and the customary social differentiation between elders, middle-farmers, and single men households re-asserted itself under the new conditions. By examining Rapitok's cash balance of payments we see that its link with the wider economy is based largely on the export of cash crops; copra and cocoa. However, cash cropping did not make great demands on Rapitok's economic resources: ample highly fertile land was available and subsistence as well as new cash crops needed little labour. New economic opportunities did not, therefore, provide an alternative to customary behaviour; rather, the inhabitants could superimpose their new cash earning activities on to their traditional life. This in turn enabled their traditional social system to survive practically unimpaired by the new forces of change. However, the increasing rate of cash crop expansion coupled with a rapidly growing population produced a scarcity

* 'Parish' denotes the largest local group forming a political unit (see Hogbin and Wedgwood, 1953:243).

of land, more so each year. This began to undermine the traditional social organisation. The existence of large capital assets, such as trucks and copra driers, as well as large areas under perennial cash crops, affected in particular the customary system of matrilineal inheritance. Conversely matrilineal inheritance affected economic growth.

In Chapter 6 I discuss the Tolai Cocoa Project and point out the connection between the drift away from the project and the system of matrilineal inheritance. In Chapter 7 I discuss Tolai trade at Rabaul market. I outline the complete absence of competition at this market, in spite of the large number of small sellers and the large number of small buyers. I attempt to attribute this to the lack of professional traders, which in turn, I suggest, was due to comparative wealth and a highly integrated society. Finally, in the concluding chapter I discuss the theoretical implications arising out of this study of Tolai economic development. I end by making a few practical suggestions to further economic growth in small-scale underdeveloped societies.

In the course of this book I give evidence of Tolai rapid economic expansion and the form this has taken. I examine the indigenous social and economic factors as well as the external variables involved, which facilitated their economic growth. Furthermore, I outline how much, and in what aspects, the traditional social system has changed, or is likely to change, in the process of economic expansion.

Capitalism, Primitive and Modern

I

The Tolai Scene

European discovery of the Bismarck Archipelago, of which New Britain is the largest island, can be attributed to Dampier who, in 1699, sailed through the straits separating New Britain from New Guinea. Until then New Britain and the whole of the Bismarck Archipelago had been regarded as part of New Guinea. In 1767 Carteret sailed through St George's Channel and established the separate entity of New Britain and New Ireland. Blanche Bay, where Rabaul is situated, was discovered by the English warship *Blanche* as late as 1872, and Simpson Harbour was named after her captain.

The Area

The Gazelle Peninsula, called after the German scientific exploration vessel *Gazelle* which operated in the area in 1877, occupies the north-east corner of New Britain. The Tolai reside on the northern coastal tip of the peninsula, in an area of about 300 square miles. About 40 per cent of this area was alienated by the German administration to foreign interests prior to the first world war and is still under expatriate control. Topographically, geologically, and ethnologically the Gazelle Peninsula differs sharply from the rest of New Britain: its coastline is straighter and steeper; hills rise from within 1,000 yards of the shore on all sides, except at Rabaul where the coastal plain is wider. The Tolai area of settlement is flanked by natural borders: to the north and east by the sea and to the south and west by a broad valley which separates it from the rugged Baining Mountains. Except for sporadic contacts, mainly with the neighbouring autochtonous Baining people and with smaller groups such as the Butams, Taulils, and others, who lived on the fringe of the area, the Tolai were effectively isolated from contact by land with the rest of the island.

The Bismarck Archipelago is an area of recent uplift, in essence a series of mountain chains in the course of emergence. Both in New Britain and in southern New Ireland the processes of uplift and erosion have advanced sufficiently to expose a core of crystalline and metamorphic rocks of the Mesozoic period, on the flanks of which are disposed more recent Tertiary and Quaternary formations — mudstones, limestones, and, especially, volcanics. South of the Gazelle Peninsula, towards Wide Bay, is the Mesozoic and early Tertiary massif of Mt Sinewit; westwards are crystalline rocks of uncertain age exposed in the core of the rugged Baining Mountains (see Map I).

The Gazelle Peninsula itself, however, is formed mainly of Quaternary intermediate and basic volcanics, together with some alluvial and colluvial formations. Blanche Bay and the inner basin of Simpson Harbour are the sites of ancient submerged volcanic cones (calderas), which have arisen through the cataclysmic eruption or foundering of the centres of the volcanoes, leaving only the outer slopes. These outer slopes fall away from Simpson Harbour to the lowlands of the Warangoi valley and Ataliklikun Bay. The lavas are mantled by great thickness of more recent ash falls from the smaller cones, recently or currently active, that surround Simpson Harbour. The first important manifestation of volcanic activity observed by Europeans was in 1878. Dr George Brown, the first missionary in the area and a distinguished naturalist, gives a vivid and detailed account of how a small island, Vulcan Island, suddenly emerged in the middle of Blanche Bay (1908: 240). During the major eruption in 1937, when first Vulcan and then Tavuvur erupted, Vulcan Island was joined to the mainland by deposits of ash, and considerable deposits of fragmentary material were spread over a wide area (Andrews, 1957:25). Rabaul is surrounded by young volcanic rocks and the whole region is covered by volcanic ash deposits, which account for the high fertility of the soils.

Seasonal variations in temperature are negligible on the Gazelle Peninsula. The average annual temperature is 79°F.;

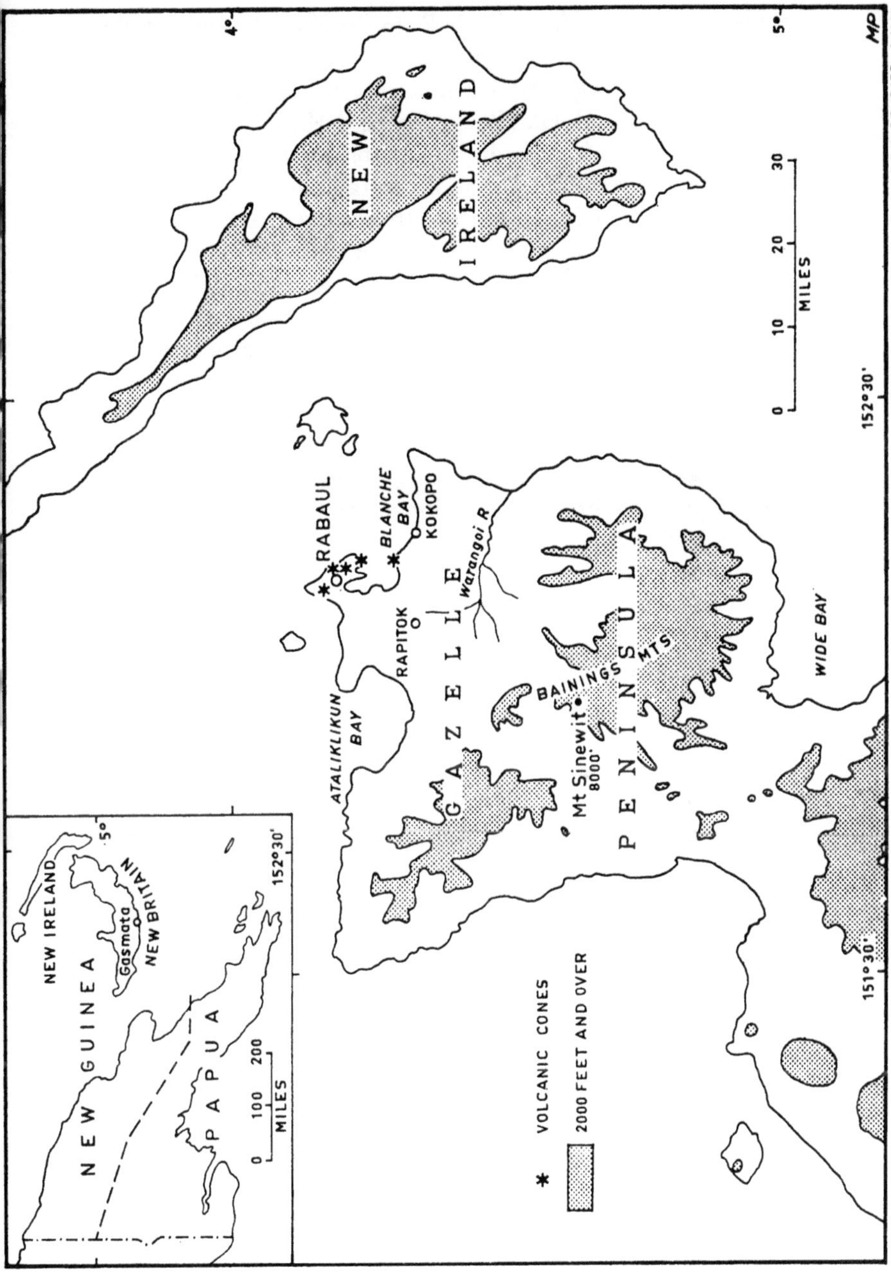

I *The Gazelle Peninsula and adjacent areas*

temperatures range from 78·1°F. to 79·3°F. throughout the year (Braak, 1931:108). Humidity in the area is high at all seasons: the average relative humidity in Rabaul is 76 per cent (Geographical Handbook Series, 1945:91). Seasons in New Britain are primarily distinguishable by the changes in the winds and the resultant variations in rainfall. The Tolai area is the driest part of the island, with average rainfalls varying from 78 in. (Rabaul aerodrome, 17 years), and 77 in. (Kokopo, 28 years), to 88 in. (Rabaul town, 27 years) and 239 in. (Gasmata, 21 years) (see Map I). The marked seasonal fluctuations characteristic of most of New Britain are absent in this area, though rainfall is least between July and October and greatest between December and March. Long spells of either dry or wet weather are comparatively unusual. In view of the high porosity of the volcanic ash soils, this moderate and equable rainfall provides growing conditions for crops in which the soils are seldom overwet and there is little risk of drought. There is therefore little seasonal variation in Tolai agriculture; most crops can be planted and harvested at any time of the year.

The Gazelle Peninsula and the whole of New Britain originally had vegetation similar to that of the Solomon Islands and the adjoining parts of New Guinea. However, this has been much altered by human influence. At one time the whole of the island was covered by luxuriant rain-forest, except on newly deposited volcanic ash where trees had not had time to establish themselves. Today most of the old forests have been destroyed by shifting cultivation and the land is either under cultivation or under secondary rain-forest, thickets of brambles, or kunai grass. All the common crop plants of the Western Pacific, such as coconuts, yams, taro, sweet potatoes, sugar cane, have been traditionally cultivated by the Tolai. Like most Melanesians, they have a great love for flowers and plants with ornamental leaves. Round hamlets and along tracks, *Crotons, Hibiscus,* and other shrubs and trees such as the scarlet-flowered *Delonix (Poinciana regia)* and the variegated *Erythrina*, are commonly planted and make splashes of bright colour. The colourful leaves and blossoms provide the Tolai with means to decorate themselves not only on festive occasions, but also everyday. I have often seen men or women on their way to their gardens picking up brightly coloured leaves or flowers and sticking them into their hair. Another source of ornamentation is the brightly coloured feathers of parrots, cockatoos, and lories which are abundant in the area.

In pre-European times, this environment provided ample natural resources from which wealth could be won without undue effort. The hazards were few. Droughts and floods were rare, and earthquakes, though common, were seldom severe enough to do much structural damage or cause landslides. More serious were the violent eruptions of the volcanoes around Simpson Harbour, which, if they did ultimately provide beneficial top-dressings to the soils, also destroyed crops and trees under the fall of ash.

In modern times another feature has become of major significance in the lives of the people: Simpson Harbour provides a large, deep, and completely sheltered haven that is among the best in the South Pacific, strategically located near the strait between New Britain and New Ireland and central to a wide area of islands. The advantages of this harbour were perceived by Japanese invaders who made Rabaul the principal base of their operations in the south-west Pacific between 1942 and 1944. The second largest town in Papua-New Guinea has grown up in the Tolai area not only because of the fertility of the environment and the comparatively high degree of economic development of the Gazelle Peninsula but also because of the strategic location and natural advantages of Simpson Harbour as the main seaport of the Bismarck Archipelago.

The People

The Tolai are a people of Melanesian stock, who in 1960 numbered about 40,000. They are culturally and linguistically fairly homogeneous, except for minor differences in dialect, and are thus a large group by Melanesian standards. Nevertheless, they had no traditional system of centralised authority. Political organisation was centred on the parish *(gunan)*, within which were situated a number of small hamlets *(iklik na gunan)*. A hamlet usually consisted of two or three households made up of a set of brothers with their wives and children, or a married man with his immediate family as well as his uterine nephews with their families, or of a three-generation patrilineal family unit. The number and size of hamlets in each parish varied greatly according to the density of settlement. Each hamlet, in fact each piece of land cultivated within memory, had clearly defined boundaries and bore its own distinct name, usually of a tree or a plant; rights of cultivation were tied up with knowledge of land names.

The Tolai are a matrilineal people who settled avunculo-virilocally or patri-virilocally. In cases of inter-parish marriages the former arrangement meant that sons, who had grown up in their father's hamlet, had to move on his death or on the occasion of their own marriage to their mother's brother's parish, where they had rights to land. According to custom, land ownership is vested in the matrilineage and the individual has a claim to land by virtue of his belonging to the particular matrilineal descent group, controlling land in the area. Members of one matrilineage *(vunatarai)* live in several parishes. A number of matrilineage sections *(apiktarai)** are centred in one parish. It was the matrilineage section, rather than the large matrilineage, which was the important unit holding rights to land. A matrilineage claimed rights to land first cleared of bush by its members. Control over lands, vested in the matrilineage section, was exercised by its *lualua* (elder), who was an enterprising man with qualities of leadership; frequently he was the man in the most senior genealogical position. *Lualuas* were important not only in the economic but also in the political sphere. A man who wished to cultivate a piece of land belonging to his kin-group could do so only with his *lualua*'s permission. Similarly, if the matrilineage leased or sold some of its land the *lualua* usually pocketed the rent or the price paid for it. He also often stored the wealth of some or all the members of his matrilineage section as well as the bride-wealth received for its women. Moreover, *lualuas* held and directed parish meetings and arbitrated in disputes. Their strategic political and economic importance often led to a struggle for power between them and aspiring men in junior positions, who tried to break away and form new sections under their own

*A matrilineage section denotes the section of a matrilineage settled in one parish. It consists of one or more minimal lineages.

control. At other times the opposite process took place, whereby small sections tried to graft themselves on to more powerful matrilineage sections. This power struggle resulted in a continuous process of fission and fusion in Tolai society (Epstein, T.S., 1964:63).

Before European contact about a century ago, Tolai society was highly segmented. Parishes were sometimes at war with one another, and at other times combined against a common enemy. There do not appear to have been any permanent alliances between parishes. Fights were frequent, but despite the hostility between local settlements there was a highly developed system of trade and exchange, facilitated by an indigenous shell currency. As far as can be known, the Tolai have always attached great importance to their shell money, and their social values encouraged thriftiness. Yet their knowledge of technology was too limited to bring about economic expansion: production remained confined to traditional goods of the types they produced for their own consumption.

European contact opened new vistas. Pacification in the area re-channelled their fighting spirit into economic competition and therefore re-emphasised the traditional prestige attached to enterprise and thriftiness. They not only sold their surplus coconuts, but also planted palms on a large scale with a view to selling their crops. Cash cropping has strengthened the ties between fathers and sons, who usually help in clearing and cultivation. This in turn has enhanced the tendency of patri-virilocal settlement. For instance, in 1960, twenty-eight of Rapitok's sixty-four hamlets had more than one household. No more than 7 per cent of these multi-household hamlets was composed of a married couple and the man's uterine nephews with their families; 50 per cent consisted of a three-generation patriline and 43 per cent of a set of brothers with their families. According to informants, patri-virilocal settlement gave rise to few problems during pre-contact days. There was then ample land and no perennial cash crops and the matrilineage of the father was obliged to provide land for the sons' food gardens. These cultivation rights also served to keep alive matrilineage claims to land, since rights tended to lapse where the land itself was not cultivated for a lengthy period. Moreover, the practice of leasing and selling land was quite common even in the traditional economic system.

The settlement of sons with their father always increased the number of matrilineages in each parish and facilitated intra-parish marriages. For instance in 1960, 70 per cent of Rapitok's extant marriages was intra-parish. The only exogamous units are matri-moieties. These moieties cover the entire Tolai area and also parts of New Ireland, though names differ from one part to another. All members of a moiety are conceived as sharing common descent, but the moiety itself is not internally differentiated and has no corporate functions. There were also restrictions on marriages between certain categories of close kin.

In spite of all the changes which have resulted from European contact, the Tolai have managed to retain much of their traditional social life. They have grown wealthy and become the most advanced and influential of all the indigenous peoples of the Territory of Papua and New Guinea, yet much of their customary life has continued unchanged. This is more surprising if we consider the several changes in administration and the competing missionary activities in the area which have disturbed the continuity of social life.

History of Contact

Several European vessels sailed past the Gazelle Peninsula during the nineteenth century, yet the Tolai acquired little from these passing ships except a knowledge of the power of guns. The first foreign impact on social and economic life occurred only with the settling of traders in the area. The first two Europeans who settled on the Gazelle Peninsula in 1872 were agents from the German trading firm Godeffroy and Sons. Though their stay was cut short by Tolai attack and they had to escape in a small boat to save their lives, German trading interests in the area persisted. In 1874 the first permanent German trading station was set up at Mioko, on the Duke of York Islands. Two years later Hernsheim opened his trading depot on Matupit Island in Blanche Bay. These first trading outposts were intent on buying coconuts in order to supply copra to a growing world market. While trade remained the major source of their income for some years, it soon occurred to expatriates that if they had their own plantations in the area, they could share in the profitability of cash crops. In 1883 the first expatriate plantation was started on the Gazelle Peninsula at Ralum near Kokopo (Herbertshöhe). German trading interests were keen to validate their claims in the area, and a year later the German government instructed its embassy in Sydney to arrange for the hoisting of the German flag in the Bismarck Archipelago and on New Guinea. In 1885 the German Emperor gave a charter to the Neu Guinea Kompagnie to administer the Territory and granted it special privileges. The Kompagnie at first concentrated its activities on mainland New Guinea (Kaiser Wilhelmsland) and sent only some administrative officials to look after their interests in the Bismarck Archipelago. Later, in 1890 or soon thereafter, the Kompagnie started its own plantation on the Gazelle Peninsula close to Ralum. In 1895 this plantation covered no more than 622 acres yet by 1903 the Kompagnie had as many as 5,000 acres planted with coconuts. Certain of the administrative functions, such as the provision of judges, were taken over from the Kompagnie by the German colonial administration in 1889, and in 1899 full administrative powers and duties were assumed by the administration. The Neu Guinea Kompagnie was paid four million marks compensation over ten years.

The new German administration settled at Kokopo, the nearest port to Ralum plantation, which was regarded as the centre of economic expansion in the area (Hahl, 1942: 23). In 1910 the administration moved its headquarters to Rabaul where harbour facilities were better. Many of the German officials learned the vernacular, since few of the Tolai knew pidgin (Schnee, 1904: 101). Dr Hahl, imperial judge in the Bismarck Archipelago from 1896-8 and subsequently governor in the area, is still remembered by some of the old men for his fluency in it and keen interest in the indigenous population. In his capacity of judge he was struck by the apparent absence of established indigenous political institutions. To ease the problem of establishing law and order he instituted a system of *luluais* (parish headmen) and *tultuls* (headmen's assistants), whereby important men were nominated as low-ranking government officials in their home parishes. These *luluais* had certain administrative and police duties as well as the power to act as judges in minor local disputes involving no more than 25 marks (25/-) or the equivalent of 10 fathoms shell money compensation. In many instances, the appointment of *luluai* fortified the already existing influence of a 'big man'. As emblems of their office, they were issued with peaked hats and staves with silver knobs (Schnee, 1904: 101). From 1905 onwards the German administration expected each *luluai* to send suitable young people from his parish for training as medical orderlies. After training, these people were expected eventually to return to their native parishes and act as assistants to the *luluai* in the sphere of native health.

To keep the indigenes working, the German government decreed that Europeans should buy only cut copra, rather than whole coconuts, and that only money and not shell should be used in trade. Moreover, a poll tax of 5 marks (5/-) was introduced in 1905 to force natives into a cash economy. When subsequently rates were increased to 7 (7/-) or 10 marks (10/-) for advanced groups, Tolai competed to pay the higher sum (Deutsche Regierung, 1911: 152).

German administrators sponsored native education; they wanted to free themselves from dependence on Chinese, Japanese and Malays for technical and low-grade clerical work (Rowley, 1958: 253). In 1906 the government started a school on Namanula Hill, Rabaul, where the cream of the indigenous youth from the whole of the Bismarck Archipelago received education in German to train them as interpreters, clerks, technicians, and craftsmen. In 1960 there were still some elderly Tolai men alive who remembered German and felt frustrated because, according to their own estimate, their early education had destined them for a better life than they had actually managed to realise.

When the Australian military administration occupied New Guinea in 1914, the Gazelle Peninsula had already experienced the beginnings of economic expansion. In 1913, 5,000 tons of copra were produced by natives in the Bismarck Archipelago (see Table 1). I estimate that the Tolai produced 4,000 tons of this. Assuming that each tree yields forty nuts and hence

13 lb. of copra, some 690,000 trees were needed to produce this amount. If each Tolai also consumed two coconuts every week, a minimum requirement indeed, then an additional 70,000 trees were needed for subsistence, making a total of 760,000 bearing trees. The Tolai then numbered 19,000, giving a mean of 40 productive palm trees a head. About 10 per cent of coconuts were consumed; the rest were made into copra and sold. At the same time there were already 2,923,995 coconut palms on expatriate plantations in the Bismarck Archipelago (*Amtsblatt*, 15 May 1914) of which probably as many as 90 per cent were on the Gazelle Peninsula. These plantations employed natives mainly from other areas in the Territory and provided a market for food crops such as taro and sweet potatoes grown by Tolai. Moreover, the German administration built an extensive road network on the Gazelle Peninsula to provide trade channels and easy access to plantations. By the beginning of World War I, the people had already come to appreciate the advantages of the new opportunities resulting from European contact. They were keen to wear clothing; some of them owned smart European suits, shirts, ties, socks, and shoes. A few educated men, products of the Namanula school, were already working as bank clerks, interpreters, printers, and so on.

The sudden change in administration in 1914 brought economic development to a standstill at least temporarily. According to the first report of the Commonwealth to the League of Nations it was in fact the Australians' aim 'to maintain the economic condition of the Territory in the state in which it was found at the commencement of occupation' (C.o.A., 1914/21:6). After Germany's defeat in 1918 the peace treaty conferred upon the Allies in occupation of former enemy territory the right to liquidate the property and interests of German nationals and companies therein. Accordingly, the Australian authorities set up an expropriation board in whose trust all ex-German properties in the area were placed. In 1920 Australian civil authorities took over the administration of ex-German possessions in New Guinea and the Bismarck Archipelago under a mandate from the League of Nations.

The Tolai took time to get used to their new masters. When

Australian currency superseded the German mark in 1916,* they, like many other indigenes of New Guinea, were prejudiced against the new coinage and preferred the long-established mark (Mackenzie, 1939:248). During the early 1920s the Tolai appear to have been apathetic in the economic sphere: they hardly extended their cultivation activities, but merely reaped the rewards of their pre-1914 plantings. Their economic stagnation correlated with conditions prevailing on the Gazelle Peninsula at the time. The expropriation board had great difficulties in finding satisfactory buyers for the properties under its control. During the inter-war years the Australian administration concentrated its efforts on the establishment and maintenance of law and order and made little attempt to direct native education or to encourage native economic development. The world crisis of the early 1930s which resulted in a severe fall in copra prices — in 1934 one ton of New Guinea copra fetched only £5, no more than 20 per cent of its 1924 price — made things even more difficult. Tolai income from copra fell by more than 50 per cent between 1930 and 1935. During the period of depression people began to look around for non-agricultural sources of income; they started to experiment with transport enterprises, retail stores, and copra driers.

Before economic activities could get into full swing again after the end of the world crisis, the second world war started. In 1942 the Gazelle Peninsula was occupied by Japanese forces and remained under their control for three years. At first the Japanese tried to get willing co-operation on the basis of their united front against the common enemy, the Europeans (Scharmach, 1960:67). However, the Tolai soon came to realise that the Japanese were in fact more demanding and much more cruel masters than their European predecessors. Occupation officials expected their orders to be carried out obediently and without delay or questioning. They ordered farmers to plant rice. Informants told me that anyone who refused was beheaded on the spot. At the same time Allied bombing destroyed many local settlements and much of the coconut gardens. As the war progressed in favour of the Allies and when finally the Japanese

*One mark equalled one shilling.

occupation forces in the Rabaul area were completely cut off, officials and even ordinary soldiers became more and more ruthless. In 1945 the Japanese in Rabaul surrendered to Allied forces. ANGAU (Australian New Guinea Administrative Unit) provided the government in the area until 1946 when the Australian civil administration took over once more. The United Nations established New Guinea as a trust territory under Australian control. Since the 1949 Papua and New Guinea Act, the Territories of Papua and New Guinea have been governed by an administrative union which yet maintains the identity and status of the Territory of New Guinea as a trust territory.

Prior to World War II, Rabaul was the capital of the Mandated Territory. In 1939 the administration decided, because of the volcanic nature of the area and their experience of the 1937 eruption, to transfer its headquarters to Lae. The town of Rabaul and most of its port facilities were completely destroyed during the war. Attracted by the excellent harbour, European and Chinese business people began to rebuild Rabaul immediately after World War II. The administration was at first not prepared to re-establish its administrative centre there and insisted that district headquarters should be at Ropopo, near Kokopo, facing Blanche Bay (Robson, 1961:143). However, in the early 1950s, the administration surrendered to public pressure and agreed to place its district headquarters in Rabaul.

The pace of social and economic development of the Territory's population in general and of the Tolai in particular, has quickened considerably since World War II. The United Nations has put pressure on the Australian government to grant New Guinea its independence in the near future. Consequently, the Australian authorities have been devoting more effort and larger resources to developing their dependent territories. This change in policy can be clearly seen from a comparison of the financial support Australia has given to New Guinea before World War II and since. Between 1927 and 1930 an annual special grant of £10,000 was made specifically for native welfare; this was cut by half in 1931 and abolished altogether the following year. In 1926/7 only £2,182 of this fund was devoted to special instruction of natives in agriculture and development of native agriculture (C.o.A., 1927:52). About one-third of the annual special grant was carried over as unexpended balance in 1930 (C.o.A., 1930:72). Before World War II the Commonwealth government expected its Mandated Territory to be virtually self-supporting. By contrast, post-war direct grants to New Guinea have increased from £2,000,000 in 1946/7 to £9,282,000 in 1960/1 and to almost £17,000,000 in 1964/5 (C.o.A., 1965:202). These increased funds have enabled the administration of New Guinea to devote more resources to development projects. Agriculture, in particular cash cropping, has received specific emphasis. For instance, expenditure on information and extension services, of which natives were the main beneficiaries, increased from £35,048 in 1961 to £165,849 in 1965/6 (C.o.A., 1965:203). As part of the extension program the Tolai were encouraged to grow cocoa and the Tolai Cocoa Project was set up to secure the production of high quality native cocoa (see Ch. 6). Moreover, educational crash programs have been introduced which have culminated in the setting up of a university at Port Moresby. Political development has proceeded at an even greater rate. The first native local government council in New Guinea was formed in the Tolai area in 1950. By 1965 there were seventy-two councils in the trust territory serving a population of approximately 880,000 people. In 1960 the first elected New Guinea representatives joined the Legislative Council. Three years later universal adult franchise and a democratically elected House of Assembly were introduced. Even by modern standards this rate of political development must be regarded as phenomenal.

This short account of the history of administration in the Tolai area clearly indicates the great discontinuities in colonial government and the many changes in administrative policy the people experienced within half a century.

Apart from traders and administrators, missionaries were the only other early European contacts for the Tolai. In 1875 the first missionary, Dr George Brown, from the Australasian Methodist Mission Society, landed at Port Hunter on the Duke of York Islands and soon extended his activities to the Gazelle

Peninsula as well as to other places in the region. He was assisted in his proselytising efforts by Polynesian and Melanesian missionaries. They soon seemed to gain ground among some coastal Tolai. Their activities were temporarily interrupted in 1878 after some of them had tried to venture into the interior of the Gazelle Peninsula, when four Fijian missionaries were murdered and eaten at the instigation of some leading coastal Tolai, who resented this threat to their monopoly over trade with Europeans. A punitive expedition under the leadership of Dr Brown soon established in Tolai eyes the superior power and strength of Europeans and thereby helped to secure the future safety of foreign life and property on the Gazelle Peninsula. Subsequently, Methodist mission activity began to make rapid progress. In 1881 there were 2,400 native converts; by 1886 the number had increased to 4,000 and by 1900, after 25 years of mission activity in the area, there were 13,000 native followers of the Methodist mission. Three years later their number had increased again by a further 1,000 (Schnee, 1904:74). At that time the Methodist mission had two main settlements on the Gazelle Peninsula, Kabakada and Raluana, both manned by European missionaries with their families, as well as a great number of smaller outstations under the control of Polynesians or Melanesians, or in some cases, even at that early date, Tolai.

The mission of the Most Sacred Heart of Jesus, with its headquarters in Germany, a powerful and influential Catholic mission in the Tolai area, was first started there by priests, members of the now famous Marquis de Rays expedition, who managed to find their way to New Britain in 1882. They settled at Volavolo but their first efforts were not very successful. In 1888 the Sacred Heart Society sent five more missionaries to New Britain, who helped to lay sound foundations for the expansion of Catholic missionary activities in the area. In 1891 the mission transferred its headquarters from Volavolo to Kinigunan (now called Vunapope, i.e. seat of the Bishop) just outside Kokopo. In the same year German authorities on the Gazelle Peninsula, in consultation with the Methodist and Catholic missions, defined the borders for activities of each of the two missions in the area, so as to avoid conflicts and clashes of interests. However, in spite of imperial prohibition, the Catholic missionaries operated also in areas which had been destined for Methodist influence (Blum, 1900:71). The many breaches of the rule by Catholics ultimately forced the Methodists to disregard the border agreement too and in 1899 the German authorities repealed it altogether. As a result of this competition between the two Christian sects, there were in most parishes followers of both missions. This, in turn, often led to conflicts and quarrels among natives (Schnee, 1904:77). Indigenes themselves had great difficulty in deciding which mission to support. Frequently, they asked German administrators to advise them. Since officials had to remain neutral in this mission competition, they would not give direct advice. They were often asked for their own religious affiliation, which was taken as a guide in the native's own choice of religious adherence (Blum, 1900:82). In many instances traditional hostilities were reinforced by allegiances to different missions (Blum, 1900:83). In 1929 a third mission, the Seventh Day Adventist, entered the area. By 1960 the three missions were firmly established on the Gazelle Peninsula, and in many parishes there were followers of each. This often led to disputes. For instance, during my stay in Rapitok the European Catholic priest resident in a nearby parish prohibited his followers, under threat of excommunication, from attending weddings held by their Methodist kin and friends. This resulted in a split in the kin-group along the line of religious affiliation.

Apart from spreading Christianity, the missions' major influence has been in education. Prior to the end of World War II, all elementary education was in the hands of missions. In fact the administration was content to leave most education under mission control (Geographical Handbook Series, 1945: 197). Each of the missions set up its own system. In 1936 the Catholic mission had four training centres, twenty-four higher, intermediate or technical schools, fifty-two elementary schools and three hundred and seventy village schools; the Methodist mission, with its central educational establishment at Vunairima, had in the same year one training centre, nine higher, intermediate or technical schools, six elementary schools and three hundred and ninety-five village schools (Official Handbook, 1943:445). The much larger number of skilled and highly educated European personnel — priests and nuns — in the Catholic mission enabled it to offer higher and better education than the Methodist mission could. However, the main purpose of all education provided by the missions was the ultimate selection and training of native teachers and catechists. The secular education given by the missions, particularly in their village schools, was not of a high standard; instruction on the Gazelle Peninsula was in the Tolai language and children became literate in the vernacular only. Before World War II the educational work of the missions was not supervised by the administration nor was it inspected by administrative officers. Since World War II, all mission schools have been subject to inspection by officers of the Department of Education and all schools are obliged to teach at least oral English. The increased interest by the administration in education has resulted in an expansion of secular higher and technical education: in 1965 there were three high schools and three technical schools in New Britain run by the administration, as well as six mission high schools and one mission technical school (C.o.A., 1965: 282-3). In all advanced secondary schools in New Britain, by far the majority of pupils were Tolai.

During World War I, mission activities, even by German missionaries, were allowed to continue without much disturbance in the Tolai area. The Japanese were not as tolerant an occupation authority as the Australians had been. In the war years between 1942-5, most missionary activity under European control came to a standstill. Most of the Catholic missionaries, many of whom were Germans and therefore allies of the Japanese, were interned on the Gazelle Peninsula; they included the Bishop of Rabaul, who gives a vivid description of their experiences (Scharmach, 1960). The Japanese killed a number of Catholic missionaries and even more Methodists in the area. Some native catechists continued to hold religious services at the risk of their lives. As soon as hostilities ceased on the Gazelle Peninsula, the three major missions began to pick up the threads of their pre-war activities. They rebuilt many of the destroyed churches and schools and further expanded their missionary activities.

The history of Tolai contact with the outside world has thus been one marked by changing administrations and competing missions, set against the background of the volcanic character of the Gazelle Peninsula. In spite of this instability in their environment, or maybe even because of it, the Tolai have managed to achieve a considerable rate of economic expansion.

2

Primitive Capitalism

Many underdeveloped societies of the world have no written records prior to European contact. It is therefore often difficult to reconstruct the economic and social system as it then operated. We have to rely on reports from early adventurers, administrators and missionaries, who often over-emphasised the strange and bizarre customs of the indigenous peoples without relating much of their day-to-day life. With regard to the Tolai we are relatively fortunate in this respect: their first observers, many of them German, diligently recorded whatever they saw or heard. Thus it is possible to get a fairly clear picture of what life was like at the time of contact.

Tambu—a Shell Currency

The most striking fact which emerges from all early accounts of the Tolai is their extensive use of shell money. 'The name of this money on the Duke of York group is Diwara. On New Britain it is called Tambu' (Danks, 1889: 305). Tambu consists of small shells *(Nassa camelus)*, about 1/3 in. in diameter. These shells are buried for weeks in the ground—yellow or brown shells are not acceptable. Holes are then bored through the shells which are threaded on to rattan string (Pfeil, 1899: 106). The money is counted in numbers of individual shells, or in fathoms (measured from fingertip to fingertip, when both arms are outstretched), or fractions thereof. Tambu in fact possesses all the attributes required of a modern currency (Epstein, A.L., 1963b). It is durable and can easily be stored as small change for the purpose of everyday purchases. Larger quantities are stored in the form of coils which are made by winding strings of tambu—from 100 to 500 fathoms—around a circle of bamboo, and then covering them with pandanus leaves. These coils look like car tyres.

Tambu is an easily divisible currency: it can be counted in terms of large denominations such as fathoms or as individual shells. It is extremely difficult to establish now the relationship that existed throughout the pre-contact period between the quantity of tambu and the size of population it served. However, it is certain that the supply was severely limited by the difficulties involved in obtaining it. Indigenes from the eastern part of the Gazelle Peninsula had to undertake lengthy, dangerous and expensive trips to Nakanai, about 200 miles along the coast. There they had to trade or fight for the right to obtain the appropriate shells.

The use of shell money is widespread in Melanesia. For instance Leahy, who was the first to explore parts of the interior of the New Guinea Highlands in 1933, wrote that 'with the large native population and extensive cultivated areas we had seen from the plane, we had no misgivings about the food supply, and instead of carrying food we took shell money with which to pay for it' (1937: 152). He was thus confident, even before he set out on his expedition, that the indigenous population on first contact would be prepared to sell food for shell money and he was in fact proved right.

Some pre-contact societies had already developed to a fine art the use of shell as money. Pospisil, who studied the Kapauku Papuans, established beyond doubt that in their economy cowries and two types of shell necklace functioned as the common medium of exchange and the common measure, as well as store, of value (1963). As in modern monetary systems the Kapauku cowrie shell money came in various denominations, which had fixed conversion rates. For this money the Kapauku could buy not only food, domestic animals, growing crops, land and artifacts, but could also use it as payment for labour in his gardens, for various services (such as surgery and magical cures), breeding of pigs, the lease of land, and for damages and fines that originated from criminal as well as civil misdemeanours. Similarly, tambu was one of the main supports of the Tolai economy prior to European contact.

Yet Malinowski was rather doubtful whether the diwara or tambu could be regarded as money.

> Whenever reading ethnological accounts about native 'money' such as for example those about the *diwara* shell in New Britain or about the stones in the Carolines—the statements appear to me singularly unconvincing. Unless it is shown that the mechanism of exchange among natives there requires or even allows of the existence of an article used as a common measure of value or medium of exchange, all the data given about an article, however much they might lend it a superficial resemblance to money, must be considered worthless (Malinowski, 1921: 14).

Recently Firth condemned more generally the application of the term 'money' to Melanesian shells:

> Strings of shell disks and similar articles are certainly a form of condensed wealth and act as a store of value. But they do not consistently perform any other function of money; . . . they do not facilitate everyday exchanges, as those of food or implements, nor are market values of other commodities expressed in them. The use of such articles is largely ceremonial . . . In general, the economic system of the Pacific island native, considered apart from the effects of white contact, has not been shown capable of accommodating and utilizing a fully-fledged circulating medium in its system of production and exchange; references to native 'money' or 'currency' therefore cannot be accepted at face value (Firth, 1961: 882).

There is certainly no doubt about the important part tambu played in Tolai ceremonial contexts such as bridewealth and mortuary rites. However, both authorities quoted appear not to have had sufficient data on tambu to enable them to agree that it can be classified as 'money'. Einzig claims that even authors who are otherwise reluctant to admit the monetary character of various objects used for payment in primitive communities readily admit that the shell strings used in certain parts of the Bismarck Archipelago qualify to be considered a currency (1949: 84). He is extremely liberal in his definition of primitive money including every '*unit or object conforming to a reasonable degree to some standard of uniformity, which is employed for reckoning or for making a large proportion of the payments customary in the community concerned, and which is accepted for payment largely with the intention of employing it for making payment'* (1949: 326). Accordingly, not only tambu but also consumable articles such as rats, pigs or pork, and grain rank as primitive money. Yet even if we apply Crowther's more limited meaning according to which money is 'anything that is *generally acceptable* as a means of exchange (i.e., as a means of settling debts) and that at the same time acts as a measure and as a store of value' (1949: 20), we can readily show that tambu was indeed 'money'.

There was a high degree of specialisation on the Gazelle Peninsula even before European contact: inland natives produced a surplus of taro and other food crops which they sold to coastal Tolai and in turn bought fish, salt water, and wild fowl eggs, as well as lime, which they prepared by burning coral deposits and used as a spice with areca nuts. Kleintitschen refers to the laziness of the coastal natives, who preferred the easier job of catching fish to the more laborious work in the food gardens (1906: 100). He did not appreciate the advantages of the division of labour, of which the Tolai themselves seemed to have been fully aware. Not only did they specialise in producing different items of food, but also in cultivating different varieties of the same crop. It was noted at the turn of the last century that the Tolai

> are most observant of all growing plants. They have names for them and for every part of them, moreover, they are rudimentary botanists, in so far as they distinguish between the different species. On the Gazelle Peninsula over fifty kinds of bananas have been recognized, the difference being sometimes so small that an expert even has to be careful in their classification (Pullen-Burry, 1909: 99).

Though the Tolai area of settlement covers no more than 300 square miles, there is a high degree of local variation in soil and climatic conditions. For instance, a particular variety of banana which grows well in one area may not prosper elsewhere. Therefore, at least for the Tolai, the stage was set for an extensive system of trade by both the way in which coastal and inland produce complemented each other and the differentiation of crops produced in various inland localities and the varieties of the same crop. There was a clear distinction between purchase and barter: the word for buying was *kul*, while *buapa* denoted barter (Danks, 1887: 307). In view of all this Firth and Malinowski could be assured that in the case of the Tolai the people were not only able to accommodate a generally accepted medium of exchange; they had to have it in order to conduct their everyday transactions.

Early European observers were struck by the number of markets held by the Tolai and the extent of their trade. In 1888 a German expedition crossed the Gazelle Peninsula from Walaur to Kabaira. After two hours' walk it came to a spring where a market was held. In the course of the morning the expedition passed half a dozen other market places before it reached the middle plateau (Nachrichten, 1888: 155). There existed a chain of markets which linked the interior of the Gazelle Peninsula with the coast. The constant hostility between settlements made long travel unsafe. Though open fighting was excluded from actual market places by the institution of the 'peace of the market', those going to and from were not so protected. Hence goods travelling to or from the coast passed through the hands of a number of intermediaries, who operated at the different markets, before reaching ultimate consumers. Market values of all commodities were expressed in terms of tambu (Schneider, 1905: 30). Even human flesh was sold for shell money. Parkinson relates that on an average one human body was worth about 50 to 80 fathoms (1887: 121).

Prices for some things seemed to have been fixed, but for many articles they differed according to the state of supply and demand. For instance, when taro was plentiful it sold at one fathom for sixty, whereas when it was scarce the price rose to one fathom for fifty (Danks, 1887: 307). Not only goods but also specialist services were paid for in tambu. Magicians, expert carvers, composers of new tunes or new dances, designers of new dance decorations, were all paid by this means. The reward varied with the popularity of the expert. A gifted composer whose tune accompanied a dance performed at a large mortuary rite received considerably more than the mediocre composer of a tune sung only at a small parish rite. The organisers of a mortuary rite had to pay not only the composers of songs and dancers and costume designers, but they also had to pay the artists who prepared the masks and costumes for the dancers, as well as the dancers who participated in the performance. Each dancer received a number of fathoms which varied according to his skill: the best dancers led the performance and received about 5 fathoms each; the remaining participants were paid about 2 fathoms. The Tolai had a price for almost everything.

Danks, one of the earliest missionaries in the area, was impressed by the diligence, industry, and commercial sense displayed by indigenes. He reported that only those who knew nothing about New Britain people would call them lazy. After a residence of nearly eight years (1876 to 1884) he had come to the conclusion that, comparatively speaking, they were as busy as Europeans (1887: 315). The stimulus to most of their activities beyond meeting their subsistence requirements was the desire to acquire and accumulate shell money.

In pre-contact days each Tolai was obliged to store his coils of tambu with his matrilineage elder, who frequently enjoyed a reputation for valour, had a considerable following, and was generally feared. The elder's house was thus a rallying point in time of trouble for all those who had lodged money there. This strengthened his influence and power, for no matter what villainy he may have perpetrated, the depositors rallied round their money to defend it and in so doing defended him as well (Danks, 1887: 309). Danks refers to these tambu storehouses as 'banks'. They did, in fact, perform functions similar to those of modern banks. They were a place for safe deposits and provided channels for re-investment. The matrilineage 'banker' could utilise at least part of the deposits to finance such activities as planting large food gardens to provide for feasts and so on. Danks points out that some young men deposited their shell money with their matrilineage elder, who used it as his own. There seemed to be no redress in such cases. If the 'banker' managed to conduct his activities with reasonable success, he was then able to meet his depositors' requests, at least in the long run. However, it frequently happened that he became too extravagant and used up too much of the stock of tambu put in his care. In such instances the 'banker' was sometimes found out and discredited during his lifetime. More often, his fraudulent activities were discovered only after his death, when his kinsmen scrutinised his assets. A number of my informants told me of how their ancestors had realised only after their 'banker' had died that he had used up their own hard-earned tambu and left them broke. These matrilineage 'bankers' are somewhat comparable with the goldsmiths, the early bankers who facilitated Britain's industrial revolution.

The addition of a new coil of tambu to the storehouse took place with great ceremony. If it was the first coil of the proud possessor, the envious onlookers made mocking remarks, such as 'Wait till tomorrow, you may be hungry and then you will have no tambu to pay for food' (Schneider, 1905: 28). This expresses the customary reluctance to cut open a coil except at mortuary rites; it also indicates the importance and use of tambu in daily exchanges.

Usually a Tolai would carry ½ to 4 fathoms tambu with him as small change whenever he ventured away from home; the remainder he stored in his hut and when he had accumulated a sufficient amount, made up coils and deposited them with his elder. Reluctance to break open a made-up coil necessitated the institution of 'pawnbroking'. If a man had a coil of tambu but no small change he often asked his elder to regard his coil as security for a loan of as many fathoms as he required. Until the loan, including possibly some interest, was returned, the coil was claimed by the 'pawnbroker'. The institution of 'pawnbroking' was called *vuvuring* (Danks, 1887: 309). The Tolai were already familiar with the concept of interest. If a man had to conduct a mortuary rite and did not have sufficient ready tambu to distribute among his guests, he could not pawn his coils, because he required them for conspicuous display. He was forced to borrow. In such cases he often got a loan from his neighbour and had to pay 50 per cent interest. For other loans interest was generally 20 per cent. Time played no part in the calculation of interest; it was the same whether the period of the loan extended over one or ten years (Parkinson, 1907: 94). If a man refused to pay his unsecured debt, he was thenceforth a marked man: he was called an embezzler, his character was gone, and none would lend him shell money in future.

The economy was, therefore, even before European contact, highly monetised in terms of shell. The Tolai were not only highly tambu-minded but they also laid great stress on the accumulation of large amounts of shell money. Some of the elders are reputed to have possessed as much as 20,000 fathoms tambu. One fathom then bought sixty taro or sixty breadfruit or one small fishing net (Danks, 1887: 307). These prices illustrate the economic significance of an accumulation of as much as 20,000 fathoms.

Tambu can thus be regarded as true money. It acted as a generally accepted medium of exchange: food was bought and sold for money; it also provided a measure of value; forces of supply and demand determined the tambu price for most articles sold. Moreover, it was a liquid asset as well as a store of value: large coils represented the accumulated wealth of the Tolai.

'Big Men' as 'Primitive Capitalists'

From an economic point of view the accumulation of large amounts of tambu must be regarded as an aim in itself rather than a means to an end. The rich had hardly any greater or different range of commodities at their disposal than the poor. Yet wealth did act as a means to an end in the social and political sphere. It was associated with power and prestige. Moreover, wealth helped a Tolai to secure a place in posterity.

> A man did not go to all the trouble of collecting tambu just to be a miser or to have a more comfortable life, or to make his family richer; rather he did this so that his accumulated wealth would be distributed on his death in order that a lot of people would cry and speak of him with respect and arrange many feasts (Schneider, 1905: 36).

During mortuary rites for a wealthy man almost all of his accumulated stock of tambu was distributed as well as some belonging to his next of kin, and hence the power arena was always left wide open for new and enterprising contestants to enter. No doubt sons and sisters' sons of wealthy men were in a slightly advantageous position, since their father or mother's brother frequently tried to launch them in the struggle for power and prestige, but this support was not enough to ensure their success. There was certainly an element of ascribed status operating in Tolai society, but this did not carry much weight.

As noted earlier (see p. 6), each matrilineage section had its elder *(lualua)*, who not only controlled the land vested in his kin-group, but also stored and looked after the accumulated wealth of tambu. Theoretically, the man in the most senior genealogical position was supposed to act as elder. In practice, however, there was considerable flexibility in the system of succession. A more junior *uviana* (rich man) often managed to displace a senior but poorer and less enterprising man. Though most *uviana* were also *lualua,* only few *lualua* managed to become *uviana*. A rich *lualua* was called a *ngala* ('big man'). The *ngala* frequently derived supernatural sanction for his authority by acting as organiser of the local group of the *duk duk,* a male cult. Men, who joined the *duk duk* by paying shell money, approached the *ngala* whenever they were in need of help and protection. The master of the *duk duk* sent from time to time the *tubuan,* a masked figure, to collect fines from offenders. Fear of the master ensured the successful execution of the *tubuan*'s job (Hahl, 1897: 83). The self-made *ngala* was, therefore, not only a rich man, but also a powerful executive and administrator. Frequently he was also a courageous war leader *(luluai)*.

Pre-contact Tolai already displayed an overruling passion for accumulation. The matrilineage tambu storehouse was always guarded by several men who immediately informed the people whenever there was danger of attack. In case of emergency, men, women and children hurried there and each took loads of shell money to carry to safety. It is said that a woman pursued by her enemies would rather leave her child behind than lose her tambu (Parkinson, 1887: 105). Furthermore, 'big men' in an attempt to increase their wealth often distributed presents such as different kinds of crops, spears, clubs and ornaments among their kin and neighbours who then had to pay for these gifts on the occasion of a special feast, *vuvue,* arranged for the purpose. For the *vuvue* the 'big man' organised the erection of a special hut, which was decorated with colourful feathers. Many people turned up for the feast, dressed for the occasion. A number of them performed dances. Afterwards each man who had received a present paid for it in tambu, usually a little more than its worth. The *ngala* remembered exactly the value of each of the presents he had previously distributed and made sure the return gift exceeded the value of the original present. Then there was a big feast for all guests. On one such occasion expenses amounted to 300 fathoms tambu whereas the return totalled as much as 420 fathoms (Parkinson, 1907: 93), involving a profit of approximately 30 per cent. The *vuvue* was not simply an arrangement of reciprocity but represented the investment by one 'big man' in the form of the distribution of articles which were then generally desired by the Tolai with the knowledge of the risk involved and the intention of making a profit. Pullen-Burry reports that she heard of one *vuvue* organiser who realised 750 marks (£37/10/-) on his outlay (1909: 195). However, she does not specify the outlay involved.

The holding of the *vuvue* indicates that local markets must have been restricted in their capacity to absorb goods; otherwise there would have been no place for them. However, market trading involved tambu payments on the spot, whereas the *vuvue* allowed for credit transactions. Unfortunately, neither Parkinson nor Pullen-Burry give details as to the frequency of such *vuvue* held by individual 'big men', nor do they indicate the sanctions operating against men who refused to meet their obligations. However, bearing in mind that many 'big men' were also masters of their local *duk duk* group, it becomes clear that the *ngala* ran very little risk in his enterprise: he could, in most cases, support his secular political and economic influence by supernatural sanctions. Assuming the *vuvue* was at least an annual event, then a profit of 30 per cent on an investment that carried very little risk must be regarded as quite a considerable return. The Tolai 'big man', like a true capitalist, invested his resources in order to increase his wealth. It was relatively easier for a rich Tolai to become richer than for a poor man to start on the ladder of success. Similarly, in our own modern capitalistic society it is much easier for a rich man to accumulate more resources than for a poor man to start making his way in life.

Pre-contact Tolai, like modern capitalist society, was preoccupied with the accumulation of wealth. Moreover, people were keen to accumulate as much as possible with the least possible effort. This emerges clearly from the following account. A woman was said to possess the exceptional gift of being able to increase, with the aid of spirits, amounts of shell money deposited with her, so that double or even treble the original quantities would be returned. Numerous natives, to whom this easy and effortless reward appealed, deposited varying amounts with this exceptional woman. However, it soon became obvious that the spirits were not always prepared to work: only occasionally did they return deposits with dividends. Moreover, the depositors were given different instructions on how to make themselves agreeable to the spirits; if these were not obeyed, repayment was delayed. When the patience of some natives began to be exhausted, a few depositors were returned their money with considerable profits. This pacified some of the impatient for a while and in fact even attracted new contributors. Ultimately, however, when all depositors demanded the return of their tambu the good lady had to refuse. It turned out that a number of people lost all their deposits (Parkinson, 1907: 83). Similar accounts can readily be found of fraudulent practices by early goldsmith bankers or the South Sea Bubble or even more recent bank frauds, when men invested their wealth in the hope of big returns, but ultimately lost all their money.

From all these reports of traditional life, it emerges clearly that the people were far from being 'primitive communists', where all property was created by the owner's own labour (Engels, 1946: 180). They had in fact clear-cut concepts of ownership of resources, employment, and reward for labour, as well as of profit and accumulation of wealth. The 'big man' paid the bridewealth for young men of his kin-group, who then had to work for him to pay off their debts. In this way he used tambu as capital for productive investment. The shrewd 'big man' often got his followers to plant large areas. It was customary for him to provide food for his labourers. He recouped his expenses, plus a certain profit, as soon as crops were harvested and sold (Parkinson, 1907: 56). This was another way in which the rich man invested his resources productively in order to increase his wealth.

Since there was no shortage of land, the 'big man's' profits were in no way due to his ownership of assets, but rather they were the result of his superior organising ability. In fact each young man was given an almost equal chance to achieve a position of power and influence. The periodic redistribution of accumulated stocks of tambu on ritual occasions largely eliminated inheritance as one of the conditions of becoming a *ngala*. Every man, woman or child attending a mortuary rite or a betrothal was presented with tambu. The quantity involved, however, varied according to the status of the guest: 'big men' received most while children received least. Betrothal ceremonies of sons or sister's sons of 'big men' attracted large crowds of people all of whom received some tambu; moreover, the amount handed over as bridewealth also varied with the economic status of the bridegroom's family: the richer the family, the greater the bridewealth.

At mortuary rites the shrewd kin of a deceased *ngala* presented the largest amount of tambu to the most decrepit looking elder attending. The reason for this was that he was expected to die soon and therefore the tambu would have to be returned within a short time. There was a reciprocal arrangement as regards tambu distributions to matrilineage elders on ritual occasions. However, the richer and more influential a deceased *ngala* had been, the more people attended his mortuary rite and, consequently, the greater was the total amount of tambu distributed to all and sundry.

The distribution of the hoarded stocks at rituals and ceremonies appears to have been the only way in which the greater part of the accumulated wealth at any one time was actually used. There was no way open to a 'big man' to convert at least some part of his tambu wealth into some other durable asset; their technology was too primitive for that. All he could do was to translate his economic achievements into prestige and political influence, as well as to secure for himself a happy after-life. A 'big man's' motives in directing his resources are therefore somewhat comparable with those of the Pharaohs in the construction of pyramids; the 'big men', like the

Pharaohs, made all arrangements necessary according to their beliefs for an everlasting happy life after their death. The body of a deceased *ngala* was painted with chalk and red earth and decorated with tambu before it was buried. Tolai believed that the soul of a dead man, his *tulungiana,* travelled to heaven, *tingenatabaran,* at the gate of which it was asked by a ghost, *tolumean*, 'Where is your tambu? Where are your bracelets, that were given to you into your grave? How much tambu was distributed on your death?' If the answer was satisfactory the *tulungiana* was admitted to heaven. If, on the other hand, it could not produce sufficient tambu it was condemned to *jakupia,* a desolate place, the Tolai equivalent of hell (Parkinson, 1907: 79). According to traditional beliefs a poor man's soul was condemned to spend an eternally miserable existence, living like an animal, harming human beings, and eating dirt and rotten leaves, the worst punishment of all (Kleintitschen, 1906: 116). Wealth among the Tolai not only led to political influence and prestige but, even more important, it provided the passport to a happy after-life.

Young Tolai with enterprise, thrift, and certain qualities of leadership, usually tried to compete with established 'big men'. This frequently induced the rich men to overreach themselves by investing too much tambu in too many different activities: for instance, a *ngala* sometimes financed the marriages of too many young men and thereby depleted his tambu stocks; then when asked to organise a *duk duk* ceremony he could not realise sufficient tambu for it. He was thus regarded as bankrupt and a younger man began to take over his role of economic and political leader. Fortunes were, therefore, frequently shortlived.

A Flexible Social System

The traditional economic and political system was carried on in the same way as a card game played for chips, with periodic redistributions of the chips among the participants. Absence of inheritance of accumulated tambu wealth ensured flexibility in the social system. The Tolai had no 'social classes', yet they were obviously conscious of the existence at any one time of a few self-made economic and political leaders, each of whom had a large following of people who helped in production and sale as well as of men acting as warriors. Drive, thrift, and the managerial ability of potential 'big men' accounted for their ultimate recognition as *ngala*.

Social mobility was based largely on economic criteria. However, contrary to Marxian theories, according to which economic differentiation was determined by relationship to productive resources, social status was achieved on the basis of individual managerial ability. Land, the only major asset required for productive activity, was readily available to all and was in no way restricted to an élite. Management must therefore be counted as a separate, and most important, factor of production in the traditional economy, apart from land, labour, and capital. Thrifty and enterprising young men shrewdly invested their tambu capital productively and thereby managed to increase their total wealth. This economic differentiation, in spite of the complete absence of any elaborate tools or equipment, was facilitated by the conditions of 'primitive affluence' (Fisk, 1966: 23). As I pointed out in my discussion of ecology (see p. 4), the Tolai lived in an area of abundant and highly fertile volcanic soils, which enabled cultivators to produce, without much effort, a surplus over and above their immediate subsistence requirements.

The traditional social and economic system embodied many of the features which are usually associated only with rapidly growing economies, such as a high degree of social mobility set in an extremely flexible political system with status achievement rather than ascription, specialisation facilitated by a monetised economy together with emphasis on individual enterprise, thrift, and tambu accumulation. This favourable setting provided a fertile ground for the emergence of 'big men', who, like true capitalists, were employing their resources to maximise their profits.

The pre-contact economy can, therefore, be readily called 'primitive capitalism'. We may then begin to wonder why it was that the Tolai did not manage to raise their traditional economy out of its stagnation. However, we must bear in mind their isolated position and limited resources—there are no readily available minerals in the area. The take-off into economic growth requires the favourable combination of a great number of variables; even the countries which are now generally regarded as technologically advanced started their innovations no earlier than about 1700.

> The absence of important technical inventions between prehistoric age and comparatively modern times is truly remarkable. Almost everything which really matters and which the world possessed at the commencement of the modern age was already known to man at the dawn of history. Language, fire, the same domestic animals which we have today, wheat, barley, the vine and the olive, the plough, the wheel, the oar, the sail, leather, linen and cloth, bricks and pots, gold and silver, copper, tin and lead—iron was added to the list before 1000 B.C.—banking, statecraft, mathematics, astronomy and religion. There is no record of when we first possessed these things (Keynes, 1933: 360).

The history of even the most advanced industrialised nations of the world is marked by long spells of stagnation. The modern age, the period of expansion, appears to have begun with the voyages of exploration, which widened economic horizons. Similarly, Tolai economic growth can be traced back to first contact with Europeans and their new products which introduced new vistas into society. It was this first contact, which started the Tolai on the road from 'primitive' to 'modern' capitalism.

3

European Contact and Tolai Economic Development

The main features of the pre-contact Tolai economy have been described and it emerges clearly that the people attached great importance to tambu accumulation. This traditional thriftiness preconditioned them to capital accumulation in the context of a modern cash economy aimed at development, though on first contact it presented a considerable obstacle.

Transition Period: 1870-1895

The first European traders settled on the Gazelle Peninsula in 1872 intent on buying copra. In exchange for steel axes, knives, guns and ammunition, the coastal Tolai were prepared to give as many coconuts as were asked (Parkinson, 1887: 85). One stick of trade tobacco fetched about twenty-five to thirty nuts. These new acquisitions were traded among themselves along the traditional routes of exchange: coastal Tolai who were paid in trade goods exchanged some of these with their interior neighbours either for shell money or for coconuts. In this way most of the available coconuts came to the coast for sale to Europeans. However, not all coconut sales were based on peaceful trading: the acquisition of new weapons enabled some coastal 'big men' to subject their inland neighbours to their rule and steal their shell money as well as their coconuts. Thus the possession of guns increased the power and influence of elders, who were often also war leaders. In turn this increased the size of the political units by enabling a few men to wield greater power and influence over a larger number of people.

These monopolistic 'big men' resented any attempts by traders or missionaries to settle in the Tolai area.

In 1878 a number of coastal leaders combined under the infamous Talili to try to oust all Europeans. This attempt began with the incident mentioned in the first chapter, in which four of the resident Fijian missionary teachers were murdered. Talili's reason for his actions was his fear of losing the monopoly over the import of trade goods to interior settlements (Powell, 1883: 120). Powell, who was on the spot when the punitive expedition against Talili and his accomplices was organised, reports that a strong force of Europeans and natives managed to defeat Talili and finally broke his power and trade monopoly over parishes other than his own (1883: 144).

The first rush of demand for trade goods began to ebb away after about ten years. The people turned more to the accumulation of tambu and preferred to exchange coconuts for tambu rather than trade goods or cash. Europeans also had begun to use it as a medium of exchange and it became obvious that the amount in current circulation was insufficient to meet demands. Some Europeans introduced imitation tambu manufactured in Europe, but the results were not encouraging. Natives discovered immediately that it was not genuine and refused to accept it (Pfeil, 1899: 119). European traders were thus forced to go to Nakanai themselves, or to finance native trips, to acquire tambu with which to pay for the copra bought from the Tolai (Schneider, 1905: 19). One fathom of tambu was equated with 2 marks to 2·50 marks (2/- to 2/6), according to its price at, and transport from, Nakanai. In spite of the fact that the cost of obtaining and importing tambu into the Rabaul area has considerably increased since the turn of the century and the purchasing power of one fathom—though it is not uniform (see p. 150)—is nowadays much higher than 2/-, Tolai still clings to this customary, though arbitrary, exchange rate (see p. 147).

After Germany annexed the Bismarck Archipelago in 1884, the Neu Guinea Kompagnie, as administering authority, accepted tambu in settlement of taxes or fines. When the German government began to take over the rule of the protectorate in 1889, the German administration paid its native road workers one fathom tambu a month plus one meal daily. During the financial year 1896 the Tolai paid as much as 923 fathoms in fines. This was regarded as sufficient to pay for the construction of roads (*Nachrichten,* 1897: 50).

Insistence on being paid in tambu rather than cash or goods meant that although traders could purchase coconuts, Tolai general consumption did not increase in proportion to the increased income. In turn this meant that trade did not expand to the extent the traders had been led to expect by the first flush of demand for trade goods immediately after European contact. Consequently, at about the turn of the century, the German administration, yielding to pressures from traders, passed a law prohibiting the use of shell money in business transactions. The favourable results which seemed to emerge from this first piece of shell money legislation induced the German governor to go a step further a year later and prohibit the use of tambu as a means of payment in any transaction whatsoever. It soon became clear that these regulations, in fact, caused a considerable decline in trade with natives: Tolai were less inclined to sell their copra or labour for cash. Tambu had been a great incentive to native copra production and sales. For some time after the enactment of these regulations the Tolai refused to acknowledge the abolition of tambu from trade and tried over and over again to get paid in shell money (Schneider, 1905: 43).

In all cases, first European contact provided one or both of two new economic opportunities: the possibility of selling labour or produce or both. The coastal Tolai, who were fortunate enough to be able to sell surplus coconuts, were not keen to seek employment. Between October 1887 and March 1893, 2,163 native labourers were sent to Finschhafen; only 523 were from the Gazelle Peninsula (*Nachrichten,* 1894: 24). However, in addition there were some others from this area who had gone to work on plantations in Queensland and Fiji as well as on the Gazelle Peninsula itself.

In the 1880s, when Europeans began to establish the first plantations on the Gazelle Peninsula, natives sold them large areas of land, often for no more than a few rifles or steel axes. These land sales were made by the elder on behalf of his matrilineage—frequently without the consent of the other members. He then took charge of the rifles and axes received. The availability of steel tools and the newly introduced *pax germanica* made it easier for the Tolai to clear larger areas of bush, while the growing market for copra, as well as for food crops, encouraged them to produce more. European plantations, unable to get sufficient labour, employed a considerable number of foreign natives, who had to be fed with local produce. As noted earlier (see p. 11), this offered an incentive to local cultivators to grow more food crops.

> While in Kaiser Wilhelmsland (northeast coast of New Guinea) the natives planted hardly enough fruit and vegetables to meet their own demands, the enterprising trading people of the Gazelle Peninsula took advantage of the European demand for taro, yams and bananas and planted these vegetables and fruit in abundance; so that their women could carry large amounts to the markets. Since European settlement, the importance and numbers participating in these markets had increased considerably. Almost daily there is a market in a different place (Blum, 1900: 139).

Native copra production in the Bismarck Archipelago rose from zero in 1870 to 1,350 tons in 1884. Probably 80 per cent of this copra was Tolai produced.* These 1,000 tons of copra brought an income, valued in money, of £4,000 to a total population of 15,000 (Schnee, 1904: 27). Thus per capita income from copra in 1884 amounted to no more than 5/-. In fact payment was often made in tambu, which was hoarded rather than spent on purchases. By 1892 native copra production had risen only slightly to 2,280 tons, of which again about 80 per cent was Tolai produced. The price of copra on the world markets had fallen between 1884 and 1892. For instance, the average annual c.i.f. price for copra imports from Pacific islands into New South Wales was £13 per ton in 1884 (N.S.W. State Register, 1884: 83) and fell to £8 in 1892 (N.S.W. State Register, 1892: 61). Therefore, these 1,800 tons yielded an income of £5,400 to Tolai growers with their total population of 16,000, raising the value of per capita copra output

* This estimate is based on the proportion of total population the Tolai composed in the area at the time.

to 6/- (see Table 1).* But since the distribution of income was far from even, the actual cash available to some individuals

Table 1

Copra Production

Year	Native, Bismarck Archi-pelago tons	New Guinea[a] tons	New Guinea[a] £	Tolai[b] (estimated) tons	Tolai[b] (estimated) £	Tolai per capita income from copra (estimated) £	s.
1884	1,350[c]			1,000	4,000[f]		5
1892	2,280[c]			1,800	5,400[f]		6
1896	2,437[c]			2,000	6,500[f]		7
1913	5,000[d]			4,000	27,000[f]	1	7
1930		63,832	869,358	9,000	90,000[g]	3	18
1935		56,251	361,413	8,000	44,000[g]	1	17
1940		59,368	504,627	9,000	63,000[g]	2	13
1950		47,094	2,264,114	6,500	286,000[g]	10	0
1959		49,328	4,451,148	8,306[e]	600,000	15	0

[a] *Annual Reports* to the League of Nations (and United Nations) on the administration of New Guinea.

[b] I estimate that about 80 per cent of native produced copra in the Bismarck Archipelago and about 15 per cent of New Guinea copra exports were produced by Tolai. This constant proportion, in spite of Tolai economic expansion, is based on the simultaneous extension of expatriate as well as indigenous non-Tolai copra production.

[c] Blum, 1900: 157.

[d] Hahl, 1897: 88.

[e] Details provided by the Copra Marketing Board, Port Moresby (letter dated 3/7/61).

[f] Based on approximate prices paid by traders. According to Romily in 1881 New Britain indigenes were given one stick of tobacco worth one-twentieth of one shilling for 20 coconuts. Since about 7,000 coconuts make one ton of copra, Tolai suppliers in that year received £3 per ton, whereas its market value in Europe was £16 to £20 (1887: 15). Prices paid for coconuts fluctuated in line with world prices for copra.

[g] I estimate that Tolai growers received approximately 80 per cent of the price New Guinea copra exports realised. This proportion is based on the relationship between the export price and the price actually paid for copra to Tolai growers by the Copra Marketing Board in 1950 and 1959.

* All figures in the text are only approximate, unless otherwise indicated.

was already considerable. Many coastal Tolai were at that time interested in the purchase of European boats, and some were prepared to pay as much as £480 for one.

The period from 1870 to 1895 was one during which the traditional subsistence and shell money economy experienced the first impact of trade goods and the wider cash economy. Tolai had had their first taste of imported articles such as tobacco, rice, tinned foods, spirits, and clothes, quite apart from the new weapons, ammunition, and steel tools. Though the rate of growth of demand for consumption or semi-luxury goods slowed down for a period, the stage had been set for a rapid expansion in demand for imported articles. Since the acquisition of the new trade goods had been channelled through a few important elders, who thereby expanded their economic as well as political influence, the first European contact strengthened traditional economic and political organisation. This trend was further supported by the introduction of *luluais*, government-appointed headmen. The German authorities usually appointed one of the leading elders in a locality and gave him limited administrative and judicial powers.

By the end of the 'transition period', the Tolai had already begun to evaluate the influence of Europeans on their lives. They regarded the earlier land sales as one of the worst evils resulting from European contact. Their elders had not thought of the consequences of these land sales; at the time they had been concerned only with the acquisition of rifles and ammunition so as to gain superiority over their tribal enemies. In 1887 Tolai owned about 700 Snider rifles (Neu Guinea Kompagnie, 1887: 20). At the end of the century the German authorities passed a law prohibiting Europeans from issuing natives with spirits, arms or ammunition, and ordering natives to surrender their firearms (Neu Guinea Kompagnie, 1887: 53) and at the same time their previous land sales forced some Tolai to leave their homesteads and move to small reservations. Consequently they became greatly embittered against Europeans, and several times tried to kill settlers and regain possession of their lands by the use of arms (Kleintitschen, 1906: 119). It was during this period that they developed the feeling of ambivalence towards

Europeans which still persists today. On the one hand they were grateful for all the new interests and opportunities contact had brought them; on the other, they were envious of European business success and grieved over the loss of their independence.

Agricultural Investment Period: 1896-1930

The period from 1896 to 1930 saw a rapid expansion of coconut cultivation, which brought an increased income and at first a more than proportionate increase in consumption. The prospect of a higher and more varied level of consumption served to induce production for the market. This involved the creation of capital through the extension and improvement of agricultural properties, facilitated by the availability of steel tools. Since it takes at least seven years before a coconut tree starts bearing, the expansion of copra production involved a long-term investment by growers. In coastal areas, where European contact had been most intense, land soon became scarce and valuable. By 1895 expatriate plantations occupied slightly less than 2,500 acres. The area under non-indigenous control increased rapidly from then onwards. At the beginning of 1903 there were as many as 16,612 acres already fully planted by expatriates (Schnee, 1904: 352). In 1909 there was hardly enough ground available around Kokopo, then the seat of the German administration in the Bismarck Archipelago, to put up even a few essential government buildings. New land purchases would have involved a big expense: 5,000 marks per hectare (£100 per acre) was then regarded as the ruling price for land in the area (*Amtsblatt,* 1909: 54).

By 1913 native copra production in the Bismarck Archipelago had risen to 5,000 tons, of which at least 80 per cent was Tolai produced. Copra prices had risen considerably on the world markets since 1892. The average annual c.i.f. price for copra imports from Pacific islands into New South Wales was £9 per ton in 1896 (N.S.W. State Register, 1896: 129); by 1913 the average annual c.i.f. price per ton of Papuan copra imported into Australia was as much as £25 (Commonwealth Trade, Customs and Excise Revenue, 1913: 73). The 4,000 tons of Tolai copra yielded an income of £27,000 for a total population of 19,000. From 1896 to 1913 the value of Tolai copra output had risen from 7/- to £1/7/- per capita. Estimates of Tolai copra production since 1913 are based on the 15 per cent relationship between indigenous output on the Gazelle Peninsula and total New Guinea copra exports in 1959 for which there is statistical evidence. According to my admittedly rough calculations, Tolai copra production reached 9,000 tons by 1930. This brought growers a total income of £90,000 and a per capita income of £3/18/-. Hence Tolai copra output more than doubled during the seventeen years between 1913 and 1930 and increased more than fourfold between 1896 and 1930.

As a result of European contact, and particularly mission influence, the Tolai learned to appreciate the advantages of European goods. Accordingly, their traditional thriftiness gave way to expenditure on consumer goods. It would appear that at the outset of income growth their marginal propensity to consume was rising sharply, but it began to decline as income continued to grow.

Accumulation of tambu remained a matter of prestige, but foreign goods also became status symbols. A respected elder was expected to have a large store of tambu, as well as European clothes. Frequently, he also had a European-style house. To maintain his status he had to entertain his friends and relatives by offering them cigarettes or twist tobacco to smoke and areca nuts to chew; he had to treat them to meals of tinned meat or fish and imported rice. Thus, demand for consumer goods increased considerably. I estimate that Tolai annual purchases of these items amounted to about one-third of imports into the Bismarck Archipelago before 1914 and since then to about one-quarter of imports into New Guinea. These proportions are probably considerably in error. However, since it appears impossible to get more precise statistics of Tolai purchases, my figures provide at least a rough approximation; at best they indicate the trend of consumption growth. My calculations of Tolai purchases of clothes and textiles suggest that they more than trebled during the period from 1905 to 1913; the value amounted to about £4,000 in 1905, rose to approximately £12,000 in 1913, and to about £21,000 in 1930. By 1913 some coastal Tolai already wore white suits like

Europeans. If they wanted to dress up specially, they wore collar and tie (Burger, 1923: 153).

According to my estimates, in 1930 the value of Tolai consumption of rice amounted to £25,000, that of tinned fish and meat to £12,000, and of soap to £1,350. Since there are no price index numbers available for New Guinea during the period under discussion, and as most imports of foodstuffs originated from Australia—even as far back as 1905, 41 per cent of the total value of goods imported into the Gazelle Peninsula came from Australia—I have calculated a price index for tobacco as well as one including rice, tinned meat and fish, and soap, both based on exports from Australia, first to the Bismarck Archipelago, and later on to New Guinea. While tobacco prices between 1905 and 1930 increased only 25 per cent, my estimate of Tolai tobacco purchases suggests that they more than trebled (see Table 2).

Tolai used to smoke home-grown tobacco even before European contact, but quickly took to imported twisted trade tobacco. The value of tobacco imports into the Bismarck Archipelago increased from £7,160 in 1905 to £17,954 in 1913. In 1930 imports of trade tobacco into New Guinea amounted to £25,629. As tobacco prices increased by about 50 per cent between 1913 and 1930, these import totals imply a reduction in tobacco purchases. This is probably due to the fact that the German authorities classified all tobacco and cigarettes imported under one heading, while the Australian administration separated trade tobacco as a special item in its statistics. Since natives consumed mainly trade tobacco, it is this item of imports we have to consider.

The major part of Tolai cash income during the period 1896 to 1930 was spent on perishable consumer goods. The period of insecurity during World War I and the subsequent takeover of the administration, first by Australian military and then by Australian civil authorities, discouraged further investment, and therefore little expansion of cultivation took place during the inter-war period. As an indication of the high degree of overall economic stagnation in the area at that time we may take the fact that in 1922, when the expropriation board offered for sale 115,585 acres of coconut plantations previously

Table 2

Value of imports into the Bismarck Archipelago and New Guinea and estimated Tolai consumption of specified items

Year	Rice £	Tinned meat and fish £	Tobacco £	Clothes and textiles £	Soap £	Tobacco price index[a] (1930 = 1,000)	Price Index for specified items[b] (1930 = 1,000)
Bismarck Archipelago							
1905[c]			7,160	11,858			
1913[d]			17,954	36,081			
New Guinea							
1930[e]	97,854	49,664	25,629	83,078	5,478		
1935[e]	52,856	38,071	17,101	80,807	5,531		
1940[e]	82,308	85,633	38,455	79,590	6,959		
1950[f]	330,397	488,696	179,316	397,718	22,113		
1959[g]	765,036	836,887	235,731	615,704	93,059		
Rabaul							
1959[g]	374,344	330,343	119,187	289,255	27,462		
Tolai consumption							
1905[h]			2,380	4,000		800	
1913[h]			5,984	12,000		640	
1930[i]	25,000	12,000	8,500	21,000	1,350	1,000	1,000
1935[i]	13,000	9,500	5,500	20,000	1,400	1,080	788
1940[i]	20,500	21,400	12,500	20,000	1,700	1,520	942
1950[i]	82,500	122,000	56,400	99,400	5,500	4,600	2,604
1959[i]	191,200	209,200	78,500	154,000	23,000	4,560	3,883

[a]Based on exports from Australia first to the Bismarck Archipelago and later to New Guinea as recorded in the *Overseas Trade Bulletins.*

[b]Calculated from exports to New Guinea of rice, tinned meat and fish, tobacco and soap recorded in the *Overseas Trade Bulletins.* Rice is weighted at 40, tinned meat and fish 35, tobacco 20, and soap 5. No prices are available for clothes and textiles.

[c]*Jahresbericht über die Entwicklung der Schutzgebiete in Afrika und der Südsee im Jahre 1906-7,* Teil 1, Deutsch Neuguinea, Berlin, 1908.

[d]*Amtsblatt,* 1914.

[e]*Annual Reports* to the League of Nations on the administration of New Guinea, 1929-30, 1934-5, 1939-40.

[f]*Annual Report* to the United Nations on the administration of New Guinea, 1949-50.

[g]*Overseas Trade,* T.P.N.G., Bulletin No. 4, 1958-9.

[h]I estimate that about one-third of imports into the Bismarck Archipelago was consumed by Tolai, one-third by Europeans, and the rest by other natives.

[i]I estimate that about one-quarter of imports of specified items (except tobacco) into New Guinea was consumed by Tolai. This estimate is based on the fact that in 1959 about half New Guinea imports went to Rabaul of which presumably half was consumed by Tolai. Since trade tobacco is consumed solely by natives, I assume that one-third of all trade tobacco is consumed by Tolai. These constant proportions, in spite of Tolai economic growth, are based on the simultaneous, and assumed proportionate, increase in the consumption of specified items by expatriates as well as by indigenes other than Tolai. The European population in New Guinea increased from 687 in 1910 to 10,608 in 1957 and more and more indigenes were contacted and brought within the orbit of the market economy.

owned by Germans, no satisfactory offer was received (*Rabaul Times,* 1926). The stagnant economic climate discouraged the people from further large-scale investment in coconut gardens. The increased copra production in 1930 was largely a result of the extension of coconut plantings prior to 1913. While the rate of agricultural capital formation rose rapidly up to 1913, it decreased considerably before 1930. At the same time, rising copra prices facilitated a steadily increasing rate of consumption and discouraged Tolai from taking up paid employment. Planters had to import more and more foreign labour. It was during this period that Tolai became fastidious as to what job they did and for whom they worked, and their work became spasmodic. Consequently, they gained the reputation among settlers of being unreliable workers and 'bigheads'.

The traditional practice of hoarding tambu made itself felt also in their attitude towards money: they began to hoard silver coins, as they did not spend their whole income. Prior to World War II, any native with paper money was suspected of stealing by Europeans. Natives received their pay for copra as well as for work in silver coins, and were thus at the mercy of Chinese traders to whom they had to pay 22/- to get one pound note. Therefore, most Tolai who managed to save some money hoarded it in the form of coins, which was in line with their customary hoarding of shell money.

Investment Trial Period: 1931-1944

At the beginning of the 1930s when, as a result of the world crisis, copra prices began to tumble and consequently Tolai earnings from copra were greatly reduced, more growers looked for other sources of income. In the early post-war period pressure had been put on natives to sell their coconuts rather than process them into copra themselves. According to one 'big man', now in his early seventies, who spent his earlier life on the coast but in 1961 resided in Navunaram, a parish about 9 miles from Rabaul, Germans had paid 1 mark for fifteen coconuts, whereas Australians, when they took over, paid only 1/- for as many as 100 coconuts.* This man claims to have been the first Tolai ever to start a copra drier and tells of the difficulties he encountered in his enterprise during the mid-twenties from European and Chinese traders, as well as from the administration in Rabaul. In spite of this he persevered and finally succeeded in getting official blessing for his venture. He himself had worked on a large mission plantation on the Duke of York Islands where he had learned large-scale coconut cultivation as well as the building and operating of copra driers. His experience had stimulated his activities as regards copra drying and also induced him to travel around the Gazelle Peninsula encouraging others to plant coconuts for the specific purpose of selling their produce, and teaching them to make and run copra driers. Following his example a number of copra driers were started by natives in subsequent years, but lack of managerial and accountancy skills resulted in the failure of many of these enterprises.

Copra prices fell by more than 50 per cent between 1930 and 1935. These drastically reduced prices discouraged growers from selling their coconuts or copra. There was no direct correlation between the nut-bearing rate in indigenous production and the rate of copra output; Tolai could, and apparently did, vary their consumption of coconuts inversely with price changes of copra.

According to my estimates, copra production fell to 8,000

* The British Military Occupation ruled in 1917 that 'the rate of exchange for coconuts shall be One shilling for Forty coconuts' (B.M.O. G.N.G., 1917: 55).

tons in 1935, and income from copra was reduced to £44,000. This meant that annual per capita income from copra was reduced by more than half between 1930 and 1935. The decline of importance of copra in the total income of the Tolai can be gauged from the fact that while in 1930 the imports I selected for study amounted to 75 per cent of their income from copra, in 1935 they represented 115 per cent.

My rough estimates suggest that, as a consequence of their reduced income, Tolai consumption of imported goods fell to £20,000 worth of clothes and textiles, £13,000 worth of rice, £9,500 worth of tinned meat and fish, and £1,400 worth of soap. Consumption of trade tobacco fell from £8,500 in 1930 to £5,500 in 1935. Accordingly, while consumption of specified items fell by as much as 27 per cent during this period, prices of consumer goods fell by only 20 per cent.

Copra prices had recovered a little by 1940, and so the 9,000 tons produced by Tolai growers gave them a total income of £63,000 and a per capita income of £2/13/- (see Table 1). Estimates show that expenditure on foodstuffs rose again to £20,500 for rice, £21,400 for tinned meat and fish, and £1,700 for soap, while that on clothes and textiles remained stable at £20,000 (see Table 2). This stability in the purchases of clothes and textiles between 1930 and 1940, while purchases of other consumer goods as well as income and prices fluctuated greatly, points to a low income elasticity of demand for clothes and textiles.

After the failure of their copra drier ventures, some of the most enterprising Tolai turned to investment in trucks. But the meagre credit facilities created financial problems. The purchase of a truck requires a large amount of cash usually beyond the means of any single Tolai, and therefore members of a kin-group often pooled their resources to purchase a truck jointly. Capital accumulation was at first facilitated by the customary practice of corporate ownership of land. Like land, trucks came to be vested in the kin-group and managed by its elder. In turn, the new capital formation at first strengthened traditional social and political organisation, though ultimately it introduced an explosive element into society. The operation and management of the jointly owned trucks created certain difficulties: while the management of the new enterprises was vested in the elder, active supervision and running of the vehicles was in the hands of younger men. The divided responsibility in operating trucks led to disputes between elders and young men who were acting as drivers and mechanics and eventually induced some young men to try to buy the shares of their sleeping partners (see p. 10).

It was during this period that the first signs of a new type of political organisation appeared. The 'Young Men's *Kiwungs*' (Young Men's Meetings) were started about 1934 by young men who were dissatisfied with the way their society was developing and wanted to advise their neighbours how to arrange their lives, build better houses, send their children to school, and so on. During a period when young Tolai for the first time took an active part in the control of economic resources, we find these same men seeking political expression of their newly gained economic influence. But their political ambitions were only of a rebellious nature and did not aim at revolutionising the social structure. The young men of the 1930s are the old men of today, and their present attitudes and behaviour make it clear that they modelled themselves on the social image of their predecessors, the pre-war elders.

From the Tolai point of view, to own and operate a truck was probably the easiest and most satisfying way of making money (see p. 12). Australian authorities were therefore afraid that too many people would buy trucks and continually warned them of the pitfalls of over-competition and subsequent loss (C.o.A., 1938: 28). Since truck ownership became part of the complex of the traditional system of corporate ownership, it also became a matter of prestige for a matrilineage to own a truck. The ownership of vehicles was not simply an economic enterprise.

The growth of native income was also reflected in the increase of savings bank accounts opened by natives. In 1938 1,213 New Britain natives, of whom the great majority were Tolai, had savings accounts. Their balances totalled £9,624/18/-, with an average of £7/19/-; ten had balances of over £100 (C.o.A., 1938: 29). The continued decline of the relative importance of income from copra is illustrated by the fact that, according to my estimates, consumption of specified items in 1935 exceeded income from copra by only 12 per cent, whereas in 1940 it exceeded it by 20 per cent.

The war years and Japanese occupation from 1942 to 1944 interrupted economic development. Foreign trade in the area was practically at a standstill. When the leap-frogging tactics of the Pacific war cut off 70,000 Japanese in the Rabaul area, they became ruthless. They plundered for food and forced natives to plant large areas with rice and papaws for them. At the same time allied bombing destroyed all substantial housing, port facilities, roads and food processing plants, as well as 50 per cent of the native-owned coconut palms (Richards, 1955: 29).

Tertiary Investment Period: 1945 On

When the Australians re-occupied New Britain in 1945, they found physical and economic chaos. Yet within only a few years the people became more prosperous than ever. Their rapid economic advancement since the war resulted from a combination of factors, of which the two most important are, no doubt, the positive attitude of the Australian authorities towards native development and their own commercial drive and enterprise. During the inter-war years the Australian administration in New Guinea had been mainly concerned with the maintenance of law and order, but since World War II the emphasis has been on economic development, education, welfare, and the general advancement of the natives.

Immediately after the war the authorities injected large amounts of money as war damage compensation into the Tolai economy. Total war damage payments made to a population of 30,000 amounted to £568,847,* with a per capita payment of £19. The availability of large stocks of ex-army vehicles, which were auctioned immediately after the war at very low prices, enabled a number of entrepreneurs, who had either kept their pre-war savings hidden during Japanese occupation or received considerable amounts of compensation for war damages, to purchase trucks and jeeps.

In 1950 copra production was lower than in 1940 because

* Information received from the District Office, Rabaul.

of the large-scale destruction of palms during the war, but prices were very favourable. The 6,500 tons of copra produced yielded an income of £383,000 and a per capita income of £10. According to my calculations, copra output in 1950 was only about 25 per cent below the 1940 total, although about half the native-owned palms had been destroyed during the war. The large-scale Tolai investment of land and labour in replanting coconuts immediately after the last war provides evidence for my estimates.

The New Britain Agricultural Extension Service estimated that by June 1960, 4,150,000 coconut palms had been planted and extension of cultivation was proceeding at the rate of 8 per cent per year (N.B.D.A.E., 1960). With the increased income from copra and other sources since the war, Tolai invested more and more in trucks, copra driers, and shops. According to my estimates the value of their annual consumption of tobacco rose at that time from £12,500 in 1940 to £56,400 in 1950 and to £78,500 in 1959. During the period from 1940 to 1959 estimated annual expenditure on rice rose from £20,500 to £191,200, tinned meat and fish from £21,400 to £209,200, clothes and textiles from £20,000 to £154,000, and soap from £1,700 to £23,000 (see Table 2). Thus while prices for the specified items rose only by 400 per cent between 1940 and 1959, consumption increased by as much as 900 per cent, and income from copra rose about tenfold.

After World War II the Department of Agriculture continued its pre-war experiments in growing cocoa and encouraged natives to plant cocoa on a large scale. Before the war, Tolai had grown no more than a few hundred cocoa trees, but by 1960 they had planted an estimated 2,941,000 trees, and extension of cocoa cultivation was proceeding at the rate of 20 per cent per year (N.B.D.A.E., 1960). The planting of cocoa trees, like that of coconut palms, means a long-term investment of land and labour, for it takes about four years before cocoa trees start bearing.

Coconuts can be processed into copra by drying the meat in the sun or in smoke, or in hot air driers. Copra processed in hot air driers fetches slightly higher prices than sun or smoke dried. Copra driers, even the more elaborate hot air ones, are cheap compared with the elaborate machinery required to ferment wet cocoa beans and produce high quality dry cocoa. When the first native cocoa trees started to bear, it became obvious that their produce could not measure up to world standards while each grower fermented and dried his own beans, often in primitive fashion. Centrally controlled fermentaries were needed to make the cocoa enterprise a success. The administration, which had sponsored and encouraged the people to grow cocoa, felt responsible for helping them over this hurdle and for ensuring good quality cocoa. Accordingly, on the advice and instruction of agricultural officers, the first fermentary was built in 1952 at Ngatur. It was started with native local government funds and helped by a loan from the Department of Agriculture. This fermentary was the first really large-scale enterprise undertaken by Tolai.

Two further loans were granted to the project which brought the loaned money up to a total of £277,000. Repayment of the loans was initially fixed by way of deduction of £35 per ton of dried cocoa produced. Subsequently, the deduction has been progressively reduced so that in 1966 it was only £10 per ton of dried cocoa beans. All the loan money was utilised for investment in capital assets. During 1959 the Tolai Cocoa Project sold 917 tons of dry cocoa, which yielded a net income of £200,930 to Tolai growers. During the same period probably another 600 tons of cocoa were sold to Chinese and European traders, who had set up fermentaries in competition with the project (see Ch. 6). They seem to be able to attract about 40 per cent of the cocoa, yielding an income of £100,000. The total Tolai income from cocoa in 1959 amounted to £300,930 and per capita income to £7/10/-.

In 1959 copra production rose to 8,300 tons, which gave the producers a total income of £600,000 and a per capita income of £15. An additional £100,000 probably reached growers from the sale of food crops such as taro, sweet potatoes, fruit and vegetables. Thus the total cash income from the sale of agricultural produce during 1959 was £1,000,000 and per capita income £25 (see Table 3). Part of this income was spent on consumption of perishable goods, but a considerable portion of it was being invested in vehicles, shops, copra

Table 3

Estimated Tolai cash income from the sale of agricultural produce (1959)

	Total £	%	Per capita £ s.
Cocoa	300,000[a]	30	7 10
Copra	600,000[b]	60	15 0
Contract sales of food crops	50,000[c]	5	1 5
Rabaul market sales to non-Tolai	50,000[d]	5	1 5
Total	1,000,000		25 0

[a]See page 50.

[b]Details provided by Copra Marketing Board, Port Moresby (letter dated 3 July 1961).

[c]See page 155.

[d]See page 155.

Table 4

Population in the Tolai area

Year	Rabaul District	Kokopo District	Total	Tolai (estimated)
1883				15,000[d]
1900				17,000[d]
1913				19,000[d]
1930	16,139[a]	13,490[a]	29,629[a]	23,000[e]
1935	17,630[a]	12,736[a]	30,366[a]	23,500[e]
1940	18,262[a]	12,193[a]	30,455[a]	23,800[e]
1950	21,110[b]	18,571[b]	39,681[b]	29,000[e]
1959 (total)	35,301[c]	17,948[c]	53,249[c]	39,229[c]
1959 (Tolai)	32,047[c]	7,182[c]		39,229[c]

[a]*Annual Report* to the League of Nations.

[b]*Annual Report* to the United Nations.

[c]Population figures supplied by the District Office, Rabaul.

[d]Estimates based on German sources.

[e]Estimates based on the 1959 relationship between total district figures and Tolai population. Slightly less than a quarter of the total population of Rabaul and Kokopo district is non-Tolai.

driers, and so on. Among a population of 32,047 Tolai in Rabaul District (see Table 4) in 1959, there were 92 trucks, 42 utilities, 21 landrovers, 55 jeeps, 11 trailers, 5 motorcycles and 3 sedans. There were therefore about 130 individuals per vehicle. In the same year there were 204 licensed Tolai trade stores, and many small shops operated without a licence. Furthermore, there were twelve co-operative societies with a total membership of 6,827 and an annual turnover in general trade of £79,694.*

Economic enterprise has been adopted into the pattern of Tolai society: it has become a matter of prestige for a matrilineage to own a truck, a shop, or a copra drier. Each matrilineage is as proud of owning a capital asset as in pre-war days it was of tambu. This has led to some uneconomic investment. At the same time the lagging consumers' demand has slowed down the development of, for instance, workshops to produce furniture and other household goods. It appears to be a feature of such small-scale colonial societies that people invest in tertiary industries, such as transport and retail services, rather than in manufacturing ventures. This can be easily explained by the smallness of the home market, which makes it uneconomic to invest in machinery and start the manufacture of articles to replace imported goods. The Tolai had too little knowledge of world markets to try to produce manufactured articles for export. Investment in service industries, which by their very nature are protected from external competition, provided the only economic outlet for their capital.

During the 'tertiary investment period', formal political organisation changed from appointed native headmen, *luluai,* to elected councillors, organised into five native local government councils. In 1964 all the Tolai were united under one native local government council. Prevailing economic conditions made essential this centralisation of political authority; the necessary vesting of capital assets in the matrilineage, without proper arrangement for their management or the distribution of profits, had prevented a rapid rise in the rate of net capital formation. In order to permit a large number of people to participate as individuals, rather than as members

* Information received from the District Co-operative Officer, Rabaul.

4

Economic Change

In order to present an overall picture of Tolai economic development I have referred in previous pages to the society as a whole as if it were completely homogeneous in most of its social, political and economic aspects. However, geographically and economically the Tolai fall into three sections. First, there are those living in the coastal area near Rabaul, who in 1960 were already short of land, but are the best educated and most westernised (Epstein, A.L., 1963a). They have experienced the longest and most intense contact with Europeans and feel themselves superior to the rest of the Tolai. Secondly, there are those living on the volcanic plateau, at a distance of about 6 to 12 miles from the east coast of the Gazelle Peninsula, who in 1960 were beginning to feel population pressure on their land resources and who are eager to move to land made available to them by the Australian administration under large re-settlement schemes further inland. Whereas the coastal Tolai are reluctant to give up their homes near Rabaul in order to acquire land further afield, the plateau Tolai, who are less urbanised, are readier to move. Thirdly, there are the inland Tolai, living at the frontier of Tolai settlement, who still have ample land to expand their cash cropping.

Rapitok, an Inland Parish

To illustrate the process of economic expansion in a small-scale society, I shall focus attention on the economic and social changes which occurred among inland Tolai with whom I lived in Rapitok,* a parish situated some 16 miles south of

* Rapitok here refers to the administrative divisions of Rapitok Nos. 1, 2 and 3.

of a particular kin-group in the formation of cap
owned and operated as co-operatives or joint stock c
they had to be freed from the controlling interest of
ditional leaders. This was attempted by the transfer
political power, vested usually in the matrilineage elc
elected councillors. Though the formation of council
a direct result of prevailing economic needs—th
political considerations, such as training in self-gove
it certainly facilitated a faster rate of economic grov
the Tolai Cocoa Project could not have been ui
without the previous concentration of political pow
councils. The formation of elected councils dispersed
power among the electorate and at the same time c
political organisation. Similarly, participation in
ventures became more widespread and capital format
concentrated in the hands of a few. However, since
ditional system whereby land is vested in the mat
still prevails, informal political power is largely v
matrilineage section elders. Although many Tolai alrea
plain of the economic and political burden this system
on them, it will probably be changed only when the
elders have died and are replaced by a new gener
post-war educated men, holding different sets of val
attitudes.

Rabaul on a mountain ridge along the fringe of Tolai settlement (see Map II). It borders the Taulil, another linguistic group with whom the inhabitants were engaged in continuous warfare during pre-contact days. There are still living in Rapitok a few men who are known to be descendants of captured Taulil women who were married by their Tolai masters and settled there. Their children were, for all practical purposes, regarded as belonging to their fathers' matrilineage. Sons were readily allowed to cultivate land belonging to their fathers' kin-group. The readiness to accept descendants of outsiders illustrates an important factor in economic growth: fertile land must have been abundant in the area. In fact, leaders tried to raise their status through gathering a following by conquest of neighbouring peoples. Men, rather than lands, were scarce. However, by no means all captives were fortunate enough to be allowed to settle among their conquerors. My Rapitok cook recited a song which he learned from his father, which was sung when they were dancing around a tied-up captive before finally killing him; they were making claims to parts of his body by pointing to them. Cannibalism was a general practice among pre-contact Tolai (Schnee, 1904: 105).

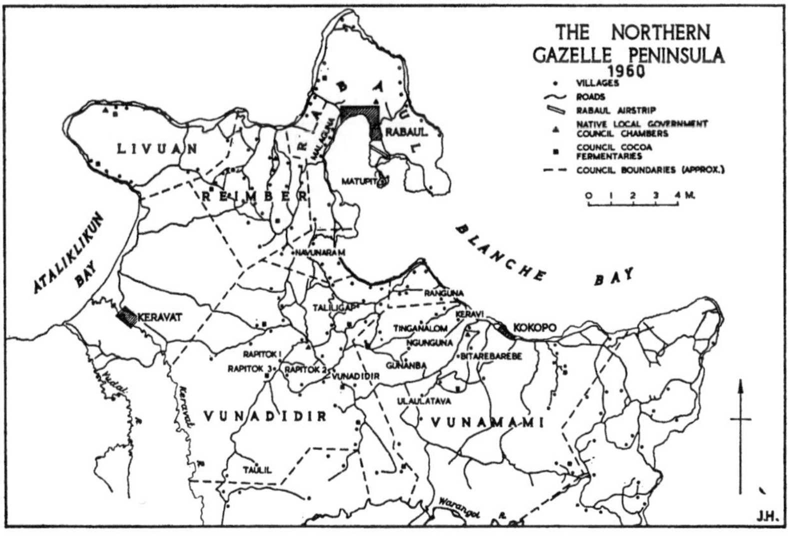

II *The northern Gazelle Peninsula*

Rapitok receives casual mention in Parkinson's classic account of the region (1907: 173). Its contact with Europeans has been peripheral and even today it is referred to by coastal Tolai as a *gunan na pui,* a bush parish. Its inland position protected it from land alienation by Europeans and it is at present probably one of the most fortunate parishes as regards the availability of land. Rapitok's inaccessability during German times may be gauged by a report on native taxation which stated that the two Taulil parishes (only about 3 miles further inland than Rapitok) could not be considered for tax collection. Their isolated position, far inland, about one day's journey to the nearest trading station, made the sale of their produce practically impossible (*Amtsblatt,* 1910). Very similar conditions probably also applied to Rapitok. A road connecting Taulil with Vunadadir and Rabaul and passing through Rapitok was built in 1910. During pre-contact days Rapitok hamlets were situated on a strategic and easily defensible ridge. The road, built after the cessation of warfare, offered easier access to other parishes as well as to trading stations and therefore attracted people to settle by the roadside. Today most hamlets are strung along the main as well as subsidiary feeder roads. In 1960 a total population of 651 (see Table 5) lived in sixty-

Table 5

Age and sex structure, Rapitok, 1960

Age	Male		Female		Total	
	No.	%	No.	%	No.	%
0 - 4	68	21	80	25	148	23
5 - 9	56	17	44	14	100	16
10-14	34	10	38	12	72	11
15-19	19	6	17	5	36	5
20-24	38	11	31	9	69	11
25-29	28	8	27	9	55	9
30-34	22	7	19	6	41	6
35-39	24	8	25	8	49	7
40-44	17	5	15	5	32	5
45-49	6	2	12	4	18	3
50-54	3	1	8	2	11	1
55-59	7	2	2	–	9	1
60 and over	6	2	5	1	11	2
Total	328	100	323	100	651	100

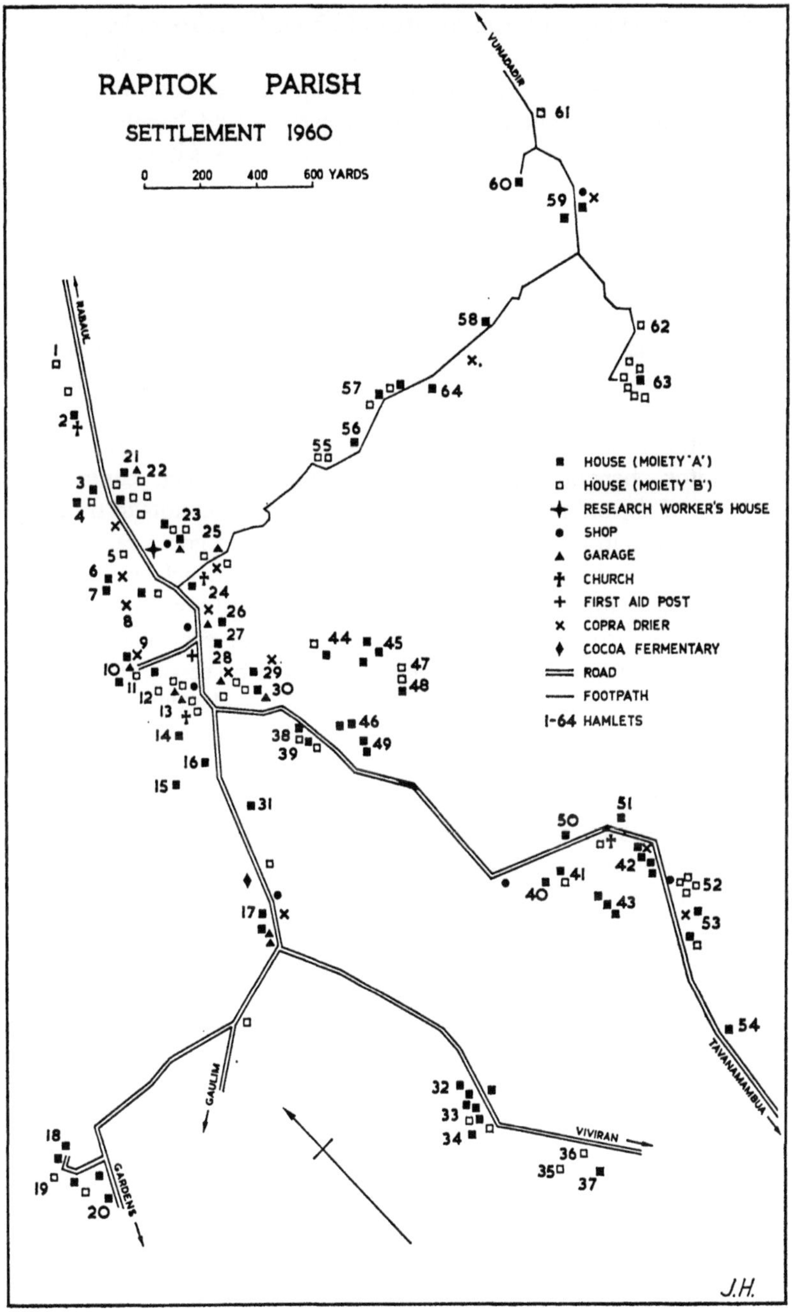

III *Rapitok parish settlement, 1960*

four hamlets spread over an area of about 2 square miles (see Map III). The old German-built dirt road still provided the only link with Rabaul; after heavy rains it was often in such poor condition that even trucks or jeeps could hardly pass. Rapitok's remoteness and difficulty of access makes its economic development an interesting study.

Labour Migration and Indigenous Entrepreneurs

As I have shown, the first European traders, intent on exporting copra, found the coastal Tolai eager to sell their coconuts either for new weapons, trade goods, or shell money (see p. 34). The returns from the sale of coconuts, which they could easily spare, were in the first instance regarded as windfall profits. The more remote inland settlements, such as Rapitok, benefited only indirectly from European contact. None of the old men remembered any sale of coconuts to trading stations in German times. The first imported goods reached Rapitok along the chain of indigenous markets which stretched all the way inland from the coast. Until a road was built and transport introduced, the sale of coconuts, or even copra, at coastal trading stations was not a practical or economic proposition. However, elders do remember a considerable number of their co-parishioners who worked on European plantations even before World War I. Whereas the more fortunately placed coastal Tolai, who could easily sell their coconuts, were reluctant to work for the new European settlers (*Nachrichten,* 1891: 16), Rapitok men coming from the more remote hinterland were keen to sell their labour in order to be able to share directly in the new economic opportunities. This is in line with findings elsewhere. In Africa it would appear that, in the areas in which indigenous agricultural production for a market could be carried on successfully, fewer men were prepared to work for wages than in the provinces in which cash crops were a less profitable alternative (Meek, 1940: 54). Similarly, South Indian villagers, when a system of canals brought irrigation to their lands, concentrated their efforts on cultivating cash crops, while dry villages in the vicinity diversified their economies and provided services for the newly irrigated settlements (Epstein, T.S., 1962: 315).

During the inter-war period a considerable proportion of Rapitok's men of working age were in regular European employment. Of a total number of sixty-three men above the age of 35 in 1960 (see Table 5), thirty-two had worked as labourers, drivers, or domestic servants prior to the last war. Another twenty-one men already dead had also worked outside Rapitok during the same period. In the remainder of this book I shall refer to those men who have, at one time or other, been in European employment as 'migrants' and to those who never ventured out of their home parish in search of work and wages as 'villagers', though at the time of my research both migrants and villagers were residing in the parish.

Prior to World War II, wage labour was practically the only avenue open to Rapitok men who wanted to earn cash or acquire the imported trade goods they all desired. However, this has changed radically since 1945. Before the Allied occupation armies left the area, surplus trucks and jeeps were auctioned. This provided some of the enterprising Tolai with the possibility of purchasing transport vehicles extremely cheaply. Some migrants who could drive and who also knew something about repairs and maintenance of motor transport managed to get the support of their respective matrilineage sections to purchase vehicles. A number of men who had faith in the return of the Australian administration hid their savings during the Japanese occupation. Immediately after the war some of them tried to accumulate more cash by converting tambu into Australian currency; they bought pigs for 5 fathoms each from other Tolai and sold them for about £20 each to Chinese in Rabaul who, at that time, were starved of pigs and prepared to pay high prices. In this way they raised sufficient cash to be able to pool their resources and invest in means of transport. By the end of 1947 there were already two big lorries and one jeep in the possession of Rapitok men. These vehicles formed a vital link with the coastal centres of economic activity. In turn this enabled the Rapitoks to sell their crops.

The coconut palm has always been an important tree to the Tolai. Even in pre-contact days it served a number of purposes. Coconut leaves were woven into mats and bags, the hard shells made excellent drinking utensils and were also used for firewood. Moreover, the palm provided food and drink: no feast was complete without *ku,* a coconut cream relish eaten with taro, bananas, or even pork or chicken. The coconut tree always had a thousand and one uses not only in secular, but also in ritual life. Rapitok men who worked on European plantations during the inter-war period soon began to appreciate the important sales value the coconut possessed, over and above its traditional significance.

Rapitok men who returned from plantation labour began to plant coconuts specifically with a view to selling the produce, rather than for their own consumption. They set others an example to do the same. Rapitok is fortunately situated with respect to cultivation: the ash fall connected with the 1937 volcanic eruption, which destroyed many coastal gardens, hardly affected the area, nor was there much damage during the war. In some coastal settlements, most of the coconut trees were destroyed during the war (Epstein, A.L., 1963a: 193). During the Japanese occupation of New Britain the Rapitoks were ordered and instructed to grow rice. According to informants, a large part of the land was under rice. However, the Japanese authorities collected the rice from growers without rewarding them for it. One or two men, who refused to work for the Japanese, had their heads chopped off. Immediately after the Japanese left, rice cultivation ceased and in accordance with Australian agricultural policy in the area, efforts were concentrated in the coconut gardens. These already had a considerable sale potential. To facilitate the sale of copra, the people hurriedly improvised three copra driers with the aid of disused ex-army oil drums put into a shelter of native materials. These copra driers were cheap to prepare and produced smoked copra. The owners of the first two trucks in Rapitok told me that by 1950 they were each making at least two trips weekly to Rabaul laden with copra as well as with pigs and food crops. The copra had been dried in the smoke driers and bundled in bags woven out of coconut palm leaves. The total quantity of copra transported each week was approximately one ton. This was usually sold to Chinese traders in Rabaul for about 6d. per pound. The monthly gross return for Rapitok's copra amounted to approximately £200 in 1950. They also sold other crops as well as pigs which returned them at least £100 plus 40 fathoms tambu monthly. This estimate is based on the assumed monthly sale of one pig for £20 as well as half a ton of taro and quantities of areca nuts and peppers.

The two trucks also carried passengers and goods from nearby parishes for which the owners received a monthly minimum of £25 from outside. About £325 would thus be a very conservative estimate of monthly cash inflow into Rapitok during 1950, providing each of the 140 households at that time with £27/10/- available in cash per year; the annual per capita cash receipts were about £6. Since the Rapitoks could easily meet most of their requirements by subsistence production they were able to accumulate considerable cash resources.

Soon after World War II officials of the Department of Agriculture on the Gazelle Peninsula began to encourage the Tolai to grow cocoa. German planters had introduced cocoa to New Britain about the end of the last century. Some of the indigenous population did begin to grow a little cocoa in the inter-war period, but only since the last war has it become a staple cash crop (see Ch. 6). One of Rapitok's migrants, who is the most enterprising and also the wealthiest man in the parish, was the first prepared to experiment with planting cocoa in 1948. He proudly related the story of how he struggled to overcome the resistance by the elders, who had never worked outside the parish, to his planting cocoa on the land of his father's matrilineage. The enterprising migrant's mother had come from another parish and married into Rapitok. Therefore he was an outsider without any hereditary rights to land in the village (see p. 6). After long discussions with members of his father's matrilineage they finally agreed to let him plant cocoa, a perennial tree crop, on their lands. When his cocoa trees began to bear, he sold the first wet beans for £3 and with this money gave a feast for the elders, who had initially opposed his planting of cocoa but who, in the meantime, had become convinced of its advantages. However, before the first trees began to bear, a number of migrants had followed the example and also planted cocoa. The Rapitoks were selling copra in the meantime and encouraged by these earnings they were prepared to extend their investment in perennial cash crops.

Since World War II Rapitok men's cash-earning interests have become centred in their own parish. This is reflected in the much smaller number who have worked for Europeans since the last war as compared with those who were labour migrants during the inter-war period. Only forty-three out of a total of a hundred and fifty-one men above the age of 20 in 1960, that is 28 per cent, had worked for wages at some time or other since World War II. The possibility of earning cash by selling crops induced the men to stay home rather than seek paid labour outside their parish. The pull of the home settlement, fortified by the possibility of cash cropping, induced migrant labourers to return to their homes and stopped potential migrants from seeking employment outside their home settlement. This appears to be a fairly general phenomenon, unless villagers do not have to make the choice between wage labour and rural activities. Some coastal Tolai, such as the Matupis who live on a small island in the vicinity of Rabaul, can readily commute between their rural homes and urban employment. In 1960 as many as 53 per cent of Matupi men between 20 and 40 were in regular wage employment, whereas only 4 per cent of Rapitok men in the same age group were away earning wages from sources outside their parish. Of these Matupi wage earners, 72 per cent were employed within the Gazelle Peninsula (Epstein, A.L., 1963a: 197). The Matupi were able to be wage labourers while at the same time remaining farmers, and were therefore still subject to stimulus from European contact whereas the Rapitoks were tending to become more inward-looking.

In the early 1950s when Rapitok's first cocoa trees began to bear and the beans were sold in Rabaul, many parishioners, migrants and villagers alike, decided also to plant cocoa trees. When the Tolai Cocoa Project started its fermentary in Rapitok in April 1956, twenty-one men registered as growers. During that month they delivered 1,944 lb. of wet beans to the fermentary for which they were given an immediate payment of 4d. per lb., giving them a total of £32/8/-. By the end of September 1956, forty-two Rapitok men were registered with the fermentary. During its first six months operation the fermentary bought 36,119 lb. of wet beans from growers at a rate of 4·36d. per lb. This yielded a total of £656 and gave each registered grower an average monthly income from cocoa of £2/12/-. At the same time some growers were selling some of their cocoa to Chinese traders in Rabaul. I estimate that at least 40 per cent of all cocoa then grown in the parish was sold this way for 4d. per pound. Each month in 1956 therefore, Rapitok received for cocoa £110 from the fermentary as well as £45 from Chinese traders, amounting to a monthly total income from cocoa of £155. If we add to this another £650 for estimated cash receipts from the sale of copra and other crops, as well as for transport charges, we see that a minimum of £800 in cash entered Rapitok's economy monthly during the mid-fifties. This yielded an average annual cash receipt of £70 per household or £15 per capita. The estimated cash receipts—excluding subsistence production—had more than doubled between 1950 and 1956, which implies an annual growth rate of just over 20 per cent.

In an economy such as Rapitok's where most consumption needs were, and still are, met by subsistence production, an annual cash inflow of approximately £10,000 provided considerable funds for savings and investment. At this stage in the argument, it is important to remember the traditional Tolai emphasis on thrift and accumulation; this will give us a better appreciation of Rapitok's pattern of income and expenditure as it was in 1960.

Collection of Economic Data

In order to gauge economic change and differentiation in Rapitok, I had to try to quantify as many activities as possible. In 1959 I began by conducting an economic and sociological census of all the 144 households. I examined the data for correlations between economic differentiation on the one hand and age, social status, and similar variables on the other. This statistical exercise clearly indicated that social status was the significant factor. There was a clear-cut economic stratification, with the parishioners divided into (i) matrilineage section elders in whom was vested the management of the landed property and also often the operation of shops, copra driers, and trucks, in which all the kin-group members had a financial interest; (ii) middle-farmers, married householders belonging to one or other of the matrilineage sections, and (iii) single men householders. Wherever possible I collected statistics for my total universe. However, since it was not practicable to survey all the 144 households intensively, I decided to compile a 15 per cent sample which I stratified according to the three economic categories and selected randomly within each stratum. None of the single men in the sample nor in the total population had ever been in employment outside Rapitok, while 50 per cent of the elders and 46 per cent of the middle-farmers in the sample had worked at one time or other for Europeans. These proportions coincide with those of migrants in the total universe. Moreover, though the sample was based on households, the relationship between the number of consumption units* in the sample, 72.30, and the total number of consumption units in the parish, 472.80, is also about 15 per cent. These relationships indicate a highly representative sample.

I had intended to collect input and output data on the main crops, as I had done in South India (Epstein, T.S., 1962: 43). However, in contrast with India, where a few staple crops are seasonally and individually grown, the Tolai have no seasons and interplant to a high degree. This meant that in a small plot of land there were often as many as ten different crops, each plant having been put into the ground at a different time of the year; crops were harvested whenever ready and required. It was practically impossible to compile detailed statistics on the remunerativeness of different crops. However, I surveyed the gardens of the sample households and counted their cocoa and coconut trees.

I also gathered details of my sample's capital assets as well as of its non-productive property. Details of all assets were collected by first listing all items of goods which Tolai could possibly have acquired and then asking each of the sample householders to state whether he had any of each item, and if so how many, when they were bought, and at what price, as well as the extent of his personal share in them. The

* Index of consumption units: Over 15 years, 1.00; 10 to 15, 0.80; 5 to 10, 0.70; 1 to 5, 0.50; below 1 year, 0.00.

Table 6

Average monthly budget per consumption unit of migrant households, Rapitok, 1960

Income					Expenditure				
Item	Elder £ s. d.	Elder %	Middle-farmer £ s. d.	Middle-farmer %	Item	Elder £ s. d.	Elder %	Middle-farmer £ s. d.	Middle-farmer %
Crop sale:									
Taro	15 5	6	3 0	2	Food	2 12 0	22	2 14 2	45
Cocoa	1 15 0	14	16 5	14	Sundries	1 4 2	10	7 0	6
Copra	2	–	8 0	7	Clothes	6	–	6	–
Miscellaneous	6	–	1 6	1	Household chattels	11	–	1 3	1
Wages:									
Fermentary			2 0	2	New houses	11 9	5		
Miscellaneous			4 11	4	Fares	1 0	–	2 4	2
Contracting			2 2 10	36	Gift	11 2	5	7 9	7
Transporting	6 15 3	56			Church contribution	8 4	3	6 3	5
Trading	11 8	5			Miscellaneous	2 6	1	3 0	3
Subsistence:					Savings	6 9 8	54	1 17 1	31
Food	1 2 1	10	1 11 1	26					
Sundries	6 3	2	1 10	1					
Gift	7 5	3	7 9	7					
Miscellaneous	8 3	4							
Total	12 2 0	100	5 19 4	100		12 2 0	100	5 19 4	100

Table 7

Average monthly budget per consumption unit of villager households, Rapitok, 1960

Income

Item	Elder £	s.	d.	%	Middle-farmer £	s.	d.	%	Single man £	s.	d.	%
Crop sale:												
Taro						1	0	1				
Cocoa		9	5	11		19	0	23				
Copra												
produced		19	6	25		14	10	18				
traded		19	0	25								
Miscellaneous							8	1				
Wages:												
Fermentary						1	8	2	2	15	0	32
Miscellaneous						7	8	10				
Transporting		2	11	3								
Subsistence:												
Food	1	2	5	29	1	6	3	32	1	7	8	17
Sundries							4		1	6	8	16
Gift		5	5	7		4	5	5	1	3	2	14
Miscellaneous						6	8	8	1	14	6	21
Total	3	18	8	100	4	2	6	100	8	7	0	100

Expenditure

Item	Elder £	s.	d.	%	Middle-farmer £	s.	d.	%	Single man £	s.	d.	%
Food	1	12	4	41	1	19	5	48	2	16	6	33
Sundries			11	1		4	0	5	1	13	8	20
Clothes			9	1		2	6	3		3	0	2
Household chattels			4			1	1	1				
Fares		4	11	6		2	6	3		8	0	5
Gift		8	0	10		4	5	5		11	7	7
Church contribution		7	6	10		6	0	7		10	0	6
Miscellaneous		10	3	13		8	0	10	2	0	0	24
Savings		13	8	18		14	7	18		4	3	3
Total	3	18	8	100	4	2	6	100	8	7	0	100

value accepted for each asset was an estimate of its replacement value, carefully checked in Rabaul stores. Shell money was evaluated at the rate of 10/- per fathom (see p. 150). Cultivated lands, coconut and cocoa trees were excluded from the calculation of capital assets, because it seemed impractical to assess a money value for these items since cultivated lands or trees were only rarely bought and sold among the Tolai.

Budget data were collected from sample households during two months in 1960. There is little seasonal variation in the economic activities of the area, except for cocoa, for which April is usually one of the peak months while August shows slack production. I therefore chose April and August for the collection of budget data. Information was collected daily by observation of, and inquiry from, each of the twenty-one sample households. The results shown in Tables 6 and 7 represent the averages for the two months' figures collected. In order to bring the different composition of households in terms of number and age to a common denominator I weighted sample household budgets by the appropriate indices of consumption units and presented the data on this basis. Income totals in the tables represent net income; for instance, transport and trading figures represent the difference between gross income and expenditure recorded in the individual budget accounts. Subsistence production and purchases paid for with shell money were evaluated at the equivalent cash price ruling at Rabaul market. Since one of my main aims in the collection of these statistics was to discover the process of economic change and differentiation in Rapitok I compiled the data separately for elders, middle-farmers, and single men householders in each of the two categories of migrants and villagers.

Transport Enterprises

Many Rapitok men, in particular migrants, were very keen on investing in capital assets (see Table 8). At this stage in the argument it is important to remember that the following discussion is based on a study of capital accumulation at a certain point in time. From available data it is extremely difficult to establish the rate of capital formation. However, it seems highly likely that as long as Tolai continue to earn a cash income they will accumulate capital either in the form of liquid cash or productive assets.

Table 8

Average capital assets of villager and migrant households, Rapitok, 1960

Item	Villager Households												Migrant Households							
	Elder				Middle-farmer				Single man				Elder				Middle-farmer			
	£	s.	d.	%	£	s.	d.	%	£	s.	d.	%	£	s.	d.	%	£	s.	d.	%
Tools	5	6	10	–	6	19	5	3	1	17	6	20	108	14	6	3	10	16	2	3
Cars and accessories	107	7	0	14	1	17	6	–					929	5	6	25	15	14	3	4
Bicycles					11	12	6	4					6	0	0	–	14	17	3	4
Livestock	4	10	0	–	19	9	0	7		15	0	8	40	0	0	1	22	4	6	7
Copra driers	5	0	0	–	1	5	0	–					200	0	0	5	1	8	6	–
Shops	12	10	0	2	4	12	6	2					91	0	0	2	5	5	10	2
Savings: Cash	58	10	0	6	29	6	7	11		10	0	5	1,215	10	0	32	33	10	6	10
Tambu	665	0	0	78	203	8	10	73	6	5	0	67	1,250	0	0	32	232	10	0	70
Total	858	3	10	100	278	11	4	100	9	7	6	100	3,840	10	0	100	336	7	0	100

In 1960 the average productive assets—excluding land and tree crops—of migrant elders' households amounted to a total of £3,840/10/- of which one-quarter was in the form of means of transport. Cars and accessories were the only items of capital assets in Rapitok where a similar relationship existed between the values invested by migrant and village elders on the one hand and between migrant and villager middle-farmers on the other. Villager elders' average investment per household in vehicles in 1960 amounted to 11 per cent of the investment by migrant elders, and the equivalent relationship among middle-farmers belonging to the two categories is 12 per cent. The large difference in the value of car assets held by migrant and villager households can be explained by the fact that a number of migrant men had worked as drivers for Europeans in Rabaul and elsewhere and could personally take charge of any vehicle in which they invested money. Some of the jointly owned cars were run under an agreement whereby each co-partner who knew how to drive could have the use of the vehicle for a limited period of time, say three months, during which he was responsible for its running expenses while he could pocket the income derived from it. This arrangement worked satisfactorily until the vehicle broke down and needed some costly repairs, when often none of the co-partners was prepared to foot the bill. Therefore there were a number of vehicles lying around and deteriorating simply because no one was ready to invest more money to restore them to working order. The divided responsibility in looking after jointly-owned vehicles thus led to much wasted effort and many wasted assets.

Ever since the introduction of motor transport in the area, Rapitok men have been keen on acquiring vehicles. The considerable distance from Rabaul, the lure of profits, and the prestige attached to owning means of transport, have led to this. Rapitok, with a population of 651, had in 1961 four large trucks and ten jeeps which were roadworthy. This means there were less than fifty individuals per vehicle in the parish, compared with one hundred and thirty in Rabaul District as a whole.

When the Tolai first started to accumulate capital most assets were acquired jointly by all or most members of a matrilineal kin-group. Recently, however, there has been a trend away from corporate towards individual ownership. For instance, while six of the ten jeeps owned by Rapitok men were the joint property of matrilineages and were managed by elders, the remaining four were individually owned by migrant middle-farmers. Two of the four bought out their co-partners' shares during my stay in the parish. Initially, capital formation had been facilitated by the traditional system of corporate ownership of land vested in the matrilineage and managed by its elder. However, the Tolai soon realised that joint ownership of capital assets such as trucks, shops or copra driers was a different matter from joint ownership of land. In the case of land it was quite easy for each joint owner to exercise his rights to it without his interests clashing with those of his co-partners, but this was not the case with such things as motor vehicles. In the beginning attempts were made to run trucks in the same way as land had always been administered, namely each co-partner had the right of using the vehicle in turn. It soon became obvious that such management of a motor enterprise presented great problems, considering the large number of co-partners involved. For instance, in 1960, 40 per cent of all the 144 Rapitok households held shares in vehicles. The amounts individual householders had invested ranged from £4 to £1,800: 52 per cent of those who had shares in transport had contributed less than £50. The most enterprising Tolai soon recognised that in order to get the most efficient service and the highest income from a vehicle, individual responsibility was required. This emerges clearly from the following example of a motor enterprise.

During my re-visit to Rapitok in 1961, four migrants pooled their resources and bought *Iapalnabret** (Mrs Breadhouse), the fourth large truck in the parish. Each of these four migrants

* Each Tolai vehicle is given a name. It is interesting to note that large trucks bear female names denoted by the prefix *Ia,* whereas smaller vehicles, such as jeeps, landrovers or utilities are given male names with the prefix *To.* According to informants this differentiation in naming is made to indicate that large trucks, like women, work hard, whereas smaller vehicles do less work, just like men. This was certainly true with reference to agricultural labour. Tolai men did chop down trees and clear the bush for cultivation, but their womenfolk did by far most of the planting, weeding and harvesting of crops.

had had a share in other transport enterprises, but had found the arrangement unsatisfactory. Since none of them could drive they had been unable to take charge of the vehicle in which they had invested money. Therefore, they never got any of the profits accruing to the running of the transport enterprises. One of these four migrants told me of the operation of the truck in which he still had a share. Only two of a large number of shareholders could actually drive and they each had charge of the vehicle for a month at a time. Each complained that whenever he took it over from the other it was in poor condition and its tyres needed repairs or replacement. Subsequently, each of the drivers arranged to raise sufficient funds to purchase a set of tyres. So each time the truck changed hands the tyres were changed completely and the driver retained his own set. This obviously uneconomic transport enterprise was a result of the ill-defined joint ownership and management of vehicles. In order to avoid such mismanagement these four migrants decided to purchase *Iapalnabret* jointly, with each of them contributing an equal share and each supervising the running of the truck for one month at a time.

Iapalnabret had been registered first in 1953 and had changed hands four times since then. The four migrants bought the truck in 1961 for £355. Before it was fit for service it needed repairs which amounted to £41/16/-. For the whole month of May 1961 I checked carefully on each item of income and expenditure in connection with *Iapalnabret*. The truck made eighteen trips to Rabaul, yielding a gross income of £114/3/-. Total expenditure, including wages, insurance, registration, depreciation, and interest charges amounted to £78/6/4, which left a net profit of £35/16/8 (see Table 9). Assuming that this one month's account was representative of the whole year, which seems likely, the owners should have recouped their initial investment of about £400 in less than one year. Each of them had contributed an equal share to the enterprise and received an equal share of profits. None of them could drive and they therefore had to engage and pay one of Rapitok's younger men to drive their truck. The owners of two of the other three trucks could drive themselves and were also reasonably efficient mechanics. Their cash outlays were there-

Table 9

Iapalnabret (Mrs Breadhouse) truck budget
May 1961

Income	£	s.	d.	Expenditure	£	s.	d.	%
18 trips	114	3	0	Petrol	24	9	4	21
				Repairs	24	12	2	21
				Wages	16	0	0	14
				Registration and insurance (£45/1/1 per year)	3	15	0	3
				Depreciation (£100 per year)	8	6	7	7
				Interest ($3\frac{1}{2}$% per year on £400)	1	3	3	1
				Net profit	35	16	8	33
Total	114	3	0		114	3	0	100

fore considerably less. These two migrant elders each owned and operated their trucks individually.

The running of *Iapalnabret* was probably the first sign of a modern joint stock enterprise in Rapitok; the four owners had each contributed and also drew equal shares; each month one of them supervised the transport activities of the truck. However, none of the owners could keep accounts; they therefore kept no records of transactions. The enterprise was entirely dependent on the mutual trust of its owners. The slightest difference between them might jeopardise the successful running of their venture. Until the Rapitoks in particular, and the Tolai in general, learn to devise a system of joint stock companies or co-operative enterprises in which each gets a share of the profit according to the size of his investment, and which are under the supervision of a paid manager trained in bookkeeping, the trend toward more individual ownership of capital assets will have to continue in order to avoid waste. However, Tolai in general distrust inter-personal loans, largely because they suspect that the borrower will rely on kinship or friendship obligations when the creditor demands repayment of the loan. Therefore, only few intra-Tolai loans take place (see p. 106).

Retail and Intermediary Trading

There were seven shops in Rapitok in 1960; four of these were under the control of migrants, but only two were owned outright by one man. In fact 25 per cent of all households had shares in shops. Here too, as with vehicles, the vague concept of pooling resources and joint ownership made shops uneconomic propositions. Though in each of these parish shops there was a large notice saying 'No credit allowed', side by side with this was usually displayed a blackboard on which were listed the names of debtors and the amounts they owed. Pressures emanating from ties of kinship, friendship, or co-residence normally made it very difficult for the shopkeeper to deny his customers credit. I took stock of one of the shops at the beginning and at the end of May 1960 and recorded each purchase and sale during the month (see Table 10). Ten households had contributed to this particular commercial venture; their shares ranged from £1 to £25. The total monthly turnover amounted to no more than £52/13/-, of which almost 20 per cent was credit sales, while monthly gross profits came to only £12/3/-. Shopkeepers' wages, other expenditure and credit sales left hardly any profit margin. This case study indicates that many small trade stores must be uneconomic propositions. In spite of this, shop ownership has become a matter of prestige. This accounts for the mushroom growth and decline of small parish shops. On my return to Rapitok in 1961 I found that two of the seven shops had gone bankrupt and closed down while three more had opened up. Moreover, two migrant elders had started shops among the Taulils and Bainings, two neighbouring but economically less advanced peoples. Each of these two migrant elders was sole owner of his venture and sent one of his young kinsmen to run the shop. These shop managers were outsiders to the society in which they operated and could more easily resist demands for credit. Accounts for the Baining shop for May 1961 may be taken to indicate that it was more profitable for Tolai to trade in a foreign rather than in their own community. The total monthly turnover amounted to as much as £140, all of which was paid in cash; transport and wages accounted together for £9, which left a monthly profit of £71 (see Table 10). The high turnover of the Baining shop, as

Table 10

Monthly shop account, Rapitok and Baining

Income					Expenditure				
Item	Rapitok May 1960 £ s. d.	%	Baining May 1961 £ s. d.	%	Item	Rapitok May 1960 £ s. d.	%	Baining May 1961 £ s. d.	%
Sales: Cash	42 10 0	47	140 0 0	57	Stock (start of month)	66 0 0	73	154 0 0	62
Credit	10 3 0	11			Purchases	11 0 0	12	15 0 0	6
Stock (end of month)	37 10 0	42	109 0 0	43	Transport	1 0 0	1	3 0 0	1
					Wages			6 0 0	2
					Profit	12 3 0	14	71 0 0	29
Total	90 3 0	100	249 0 0	100		90 3 0	100	249 0 0	100

compared with the Rapitok store, was largely due to the small number of trade stores that were as yet in the Baining area; by contrast there were at least two or three small shops in each Tolai parish. There was therefore greater competition in retail trade in Rapitok as compared with the Baining area.

The Tolai were spreading their enterprise among their less advanced neighbours not only through retailing but also by acting as intermediaries in trade. For instance, some Rapitok men bought coconuts with tambu from the Taulils or Bainings. They collected 180 coconuts for 1 fathom tambu. These nuts were then dried in one of Rapitok's copra driers and yielded approximately 60 lb. of copra which, when sold to Chinese traders in Rabaul at 7d. per pound, provided a gross income of £1/15/- for Rapitok entrepreneurs. Rapitok, therefore, needed a greater copra drying capacity than was demanded by the parish's own coconut production. In 1960 there were altogether twelve copra driers of which five were hot air driers housed in shelters made of European materials, each of which had cost about £500 to build. The other seven copra driers produced smoked copra and were usually improvised out of disused oil-drums and put into shelters of native materials. Such improvised copra driers cost about £10 each to prepare. The difference in the price paid for hot air dried and smoked copra did not warrant large investment in hot air driers. Copra prices in Rabaul were £75 per ton of hot air dried copra and £73 per ton of smoked copra between July and December 1959. However, as a result of encouragement by officials from the Department of Agriculture, ownership of hot air driers had become a matter of prestige. This was responsible for the large investment in hot air copra driers. Here it may be noted that two agencies of the same authority pursue conflicting policies; agricultural officers encourage natives to build hot air driers, although the small additional amount paid by the Copra Marketing Board makes the investment in elaborate driers for small quantities of copra an uneconomic proposition. The success of efforts in this respect by officials from the Department of Agriculture emphasises the importance of personal contact in programs. Four of the five expensive copra driers were wholly or largely owned by migrant elders. The average investment per villager elder's household in copra driers amounted to no more than 2·4 per cent of that of migrant elders. By contrast, both categories of middle-farmers invested about the same small amount in copra driers (see Table 8). This reflects both the low cost of smoke driers as well as the non-participation of migrant middle-farmers in the struggle for prestige among migrant elders.

Rapitok migrants, in particular elders, were much keener on investment in productive assets and formalised trading than were their fellow villagers. Some villagers bought sacks of salt or quantities of tobacco in Rabaul and bartered these goods in small lots for coconuts or taro with the Taulils or Bainings. They then resold these crops in Rabaul. Each of these transactions yielded a reasonable profit. Villagers, in particular elders, were still firmly rooted in their home area. They therefore had more informal and personal relationships than migrants with individuals among neighbouring peoples. These villager elders were still trading along the traditional channels which used to link the coast with the interior of New Britain. Therefore they still acted frequently as intermediaries in commercial transactions. This is indicated in the budgets by the comparatively high figure for copra sales by villager elders. In fact only about half their copra sales was derived from their own coconut palms; the remainder resulted from trade transactions (see Table 7). By contrast, the average monthly trading income of 11/8 per consumption unit of migrant elder sample households (see Table 6) represented income from formalised trading conducted in shops. There was a considerable difference in the investment in shops by migrant and villager elders—the latter had invested the equivalent of only 13 per cent of the shop assets held by the former—whereas there was only a slight difference in the investment of middle-farmers belonging to the two categories.

Agricultural Activities

As has been shown, the Rapitoks have displayed keen interest in developing tertiary industry. However, service industries can flourish only as long as they are developed side by side with productive enterprises. Migrants and villagers alike appeared to be aware of this truth; they fully realised that agriculture still provided the base for their economy.

The total area of Rapitok land covers about 3.5 square miles (2,240 acres), of which in 1960 about 35 per cent (800 acres) was still virgin bush available for the extension of cultivation, allowance having been made for the normal period of five years fallow for lands under food crops. The usual practice was to clear the bush, plant one or two food crops of taro, yams or sweet potatoes, and then interplant the area with cocoa or coconuts. Food crops were harvested before the cocoa or coconut trees were big enough to provide too much shade. In this way 60 per cent of all the land under food crops in 1960 was destined to come under permanent tree crops. Since the normal period during which land was devoted to food crops was two years, farmers extended their tree crop cultivation at the rate of about 50 acres a year. It took approximately 100 labour days to clear one acre of bush land (Henderson, 1954: 28). Therefore at the rate of 200 labour days per man per year, it required twenty-five men working continuously on clearing bush to prepare 50 acres for cultivation. Another ten men were needed to plant these 50 acres with cocoa or coconuts.

A total of thirty-five men represented 26 per cent of Rapitok males of working age, that is, between the ages of 15 to 45. Thus men of working age invested one-quarter of their manpower per year in the formation of new agricultural assets such as cocoa and coconut trees. This involved a long-term investment.

The extent of cash cropping is clearly shown by a 1960 survey of about 50 acres of randomly selected Rapitok land (see Map IV). Of this area, 25 per cent was still bush, while 75 per cent was already garden land. This coincides roughly with the overall pattern of Rapitok cultivation, in which 35 per cent was still virgin bush. As much as 90 per cent of the cultivated area shown on Map IV was planted with cocoa and coconuts. Moreover, less than half of the surveyed area under food crops was destined for subsistence consumption, the rest was intended for sale.

Altogether of the total land under food crops only about 60 per cent was for subsistence consumption. A further 30

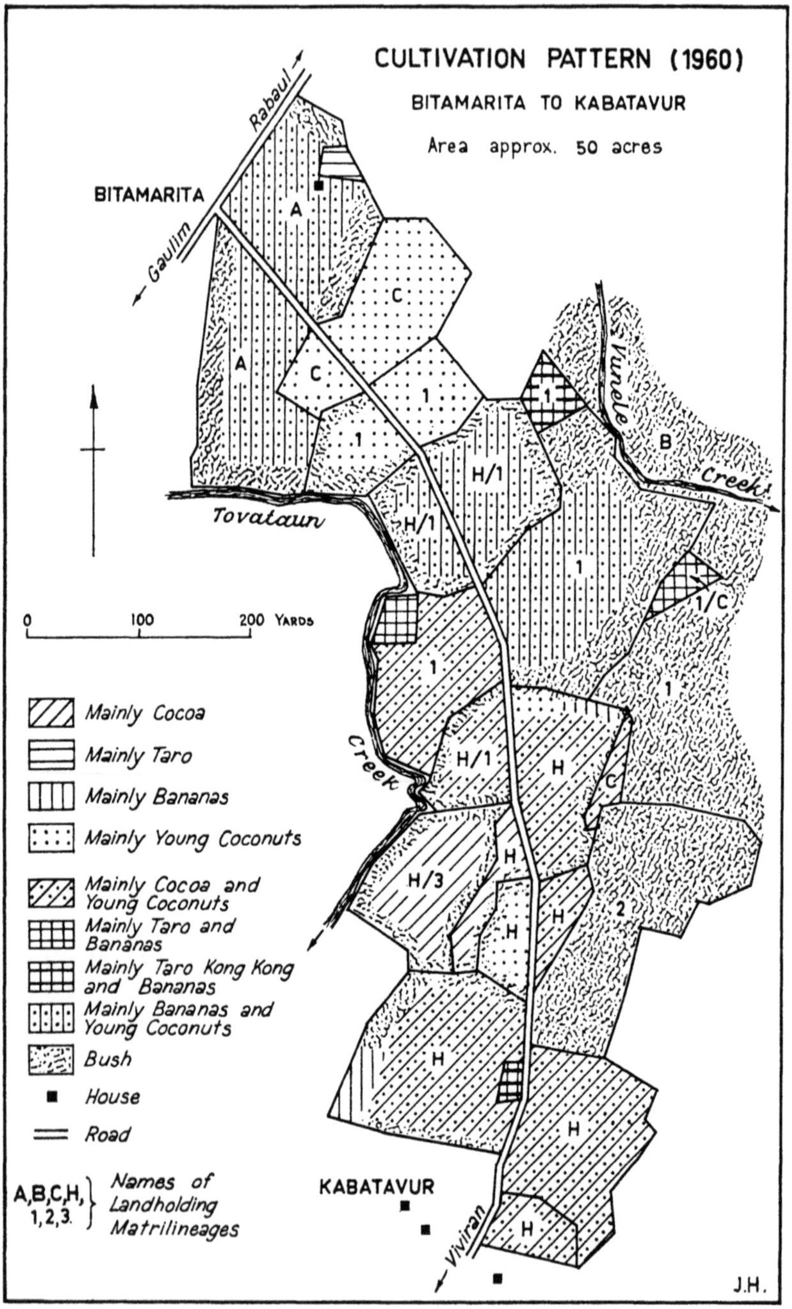

IV *Cultivation pattern, 1960, Bitamarita to Kabatavur. Area approximately 50 acres.*

acres a year were cleared for cash cropping which required another twenty men for bush clearing and planting crops. As three-twentieths of an acre provided sufficient temporary crops to feed one person for one year and each plot was cultivated for two years, only about 50 acres were prepared annually for subsistence crops which required thirty men for clearing and planting. Only 22 per cent of manpower was needed for subsistence production, while about 40 per cent was invested in the preparation of land for permanent or temporary cash crops.

The comparative annual yield from one acre of taro was £31, from coconuts £39, and from cocoa £41 at 1960 prices. According to estimates given me in conversation with the District Agricultural Officer, Rabaul, the total for taro was computed on the basis of 4,000 taro per acre weighing on an average 1·25 lb. each and fetching a price of 1½d. per lb.; the total for copra was based on 120 coconut trees per acre bearing 40 nuts each per year; each nut yielded 1/3 lb. of copra which provided a net income of £55 net per ton; the total for cocoa was based on 220 cocoa trees per acre, each bearing an average of 2·2 lb. dry cocoa per year which yielded £170 per ton net to growers.

Since the current labour such as weeding and harvesting for all crops was usually provided by women, the different labour requirements of the various crops played little part in determining what crop a man planted after having cleared the bush for cultivation. Though the relative cash yields per acre of the various crops may have had some part in influencing the pattern of cash cropping, the determining factor was certainly the administration's agricultural policy. As we have seen, Rapitok started cash cropping to a significant extent only after World War II. Although between the wars the Department of Agriculture had advocated coconuts as a cash crop, growers were now encouraged to cultivate cocoa. The success of the agricultural officials' activities emerges clearly from a comparison between the all-Tolai tree statistics on the one hand and those of Rapitok growers on the other. The all-Tolai average of cocoa trees per head of population was only 74 compared with 102 among the Rapitok population. By contrast, the all-

Tolai per capita average of coconut trees was 104 as compared with only 36 among Rapitok's population (see Table 11). This considerably lower figure for per capita coconut trees can be readily explained by Rapitok's geographical position which accounted for its late incorporation into the copra-producing area.

Table 11

Tolai agriculture

	Rapitok				All-Tolai	
	Estimate (based on sample)	Revised estimate (10% error eliminated)	Count (1960)	Per capita	Estimate[a]	Per capita
Total area under food crops (acres)	180	165		0.25		
Total area under tree crops (acres)	650	600		0.92		
Number of coconut trees	26,000	23,400	23,322	36	4,150,000	104
Number of cocoa trees	72,000	65,000	66,532	102	2,941,000	74

[a]*Annual Report 1959-60,* New Britain District Agricultural Extension dated 30/7/60.

Rapitok growers found a ready market for their products. As well as being able to sell to the Tolai Cocoa Project there are Chinese and European traders in Rabaul who are always willing to buy any quantity of wet cocoa beans (see Ch. 6) as well as copra. Moreover, the Copra Marketing Board bought copra from Tolai suppliers, provided it was packed in sacks weighing no less than one and a half hundredweight delivered to the buying station in Rabaul. Of Rapitok gross earnings derived from the sale of cocoa, copra or food crops in Rabaul, the proportion devoted to transport charges ranged from about 15 per cent for large loads to 60 per cent for individual smaller bags.

Rapitok cultivators had a number of outlets for their food crops grown for sale. In 1960 many of the bananas were distilled into 'jungle juice', an alcoholic drink produced from bananas and illicitly sold. Furthermore, two migrant elders had secured contracts with large plantations and mission stations for the supply of taro and taro kong kong (*Xanthosoma*). These contractors collected quantities of these crops from individual growers and delivered them with their own trucks on appointed days to their buyers. The grower received about 65 per cent of the gross receipts; 30 per cent covered transport charges and 5 per cent represented the contractor's commission. Rabaul market provided another outlet for the sale of food crops (see Ch. 7). Every Saturday all of Rapitok's available transport made its way to Rabaul laden with large bags woven out of palm leaves and filled with foodstuffs. Mostly women offered produce at the market, men only rarely did so. Rapitok women who wanted to accumulate tambu harvested some of their food crops on a Friday and prepared them for sale the following day at Rabaul market. Women from interior settlements appeared to be keener on tambu sales, whereas coastal female sellers on the whole preferred cash. The average proportion of tambu sales was 10 per cent of total sales at Rabaul market; 11 per cent of total receipts from sales by coastal Matupi women was tambu (Epstein, A.L., 1963a: 195); by contrast Rapitok women sold on an average as much as 25 per cent of their produce for tambu. In terms of cash, the trips to Rabaul market often represented a loss: the female seller had to pay cash for her own fare and freight, whereas her income was in the form of tambu. However, if a woman had a son of marriageable age, she usually wanted to accumulate tambu so as to contribute to his bridewealth. Or she may have even been selling crops on behalf of her husband who wanted to accumulate shell money for a feast or mortuary rite. In this way Rapitok had a monthly net gain of about 50 fathoms shell money. Nevertheless, by far the greater number of all sales these days are for cash rather than tambu.

Economic and Social Differentiation

In 1960 Rapitok villager elders owned capital assets worth only 21 per cent of those accumulated by migrant elders, while villager middle-farmers had capital assets of the value of 83 per cent of those owned by migrant middle-farmers. Thus migrant householders had accumulated more capital assets than villager householders, though the difference was only slight among middle-farmers, while it was considerable among elders. At the same time there was a marked economic differentiation between elders, middle-farmers and single men households in both categories. Migrant middle-farmers had an average amount of capital assets per household amounting to no more than 8 per cent of that of migrant elders, whereas villager middle-farmers had invested 32 per cent of the average invested by villager elders, and villager single men's households had an average investment of only 1 per cent of that of villager elders (see Table 12). The considerable

Table 12

Relationship between values of average capital assets owned by migrant and villager households in Rapitok

	Migrant				Villager			
	£	s.	d.	%	£	s.	d.	%
Elders	3,840	10	0	100	858	3	10	100
Middle-farmers	336	7	0	8	278	11	4	32
Single men					9	7	6	1

economic differentiation between elders and middle-farmers in both categories cannot possibly be attributed to age, because some of the middle-farmers were in fact older than some elders. Nor can the difference be attributed to greater enterprise among elders than among middle-farmers, because some of the latter were extremely enterprising. The one factor which could account for the difference in wealth between elders and middle-farmers is the privileged position matrilineage section elders occupied. This privileged position was apparently still exploited by villager elders and used even by migrant elders to accumulate greater wealth for themselves. Here we must remember that though elder of a matrilineage was a hereditary position filled by the eldest brother of a deceased elder or, if no brother was alive, by the eldest sister's eldest son, even in pre-contact days an elder had to prove himself worthy of his privileged position and could be deposed and replaced by a more capable man of the matrilineage. In 1960 in two of Rapitok's twenty-four matrilineage sections, the position of elder was occupied by a younger classificatory brother of the men who held the hereditary right. The latter did not possess the necessary calibre to act as elders and had therefore been replaced by their more capable younger brothers. In both cases the deposed men were pleased to be relieved of the responsibility and readily submitted to the rule of the men nominated in their place. The traditional social system had ample flexibility to allow for the removal of any inefficient elder and his replacement by one of the most capable men in the matrilineage concerned.

We have seen that in pre-contact days elders had been the pivots round which the whole social and economic life of the Tolai revolved. The 1960 Rapitok data suggest that elders still retained their strategic position in the society. They still managed their matrilineage lands and had even taken over the management of trucks, copra driers, and shops jointly owned by their matrilineage. There were, however, signs that the people were getting discontented with their traditional social system and desired a change. At many native local government council meetings, I heard councillors suggest a change from their traditional system of landholding vested in the matrilineage to one of individual ownership, so as to enable a man to leave his perennial crops and other assets to his own son rather than to his brother or sister's son. Individual ownership of land would have the additional advantage of enabling the owner to mortgage or sell his land as he wished. Yet the task of changing the system of landholding had so far proved insuperable since such a change would undermine the very basis of the whole social structure (see p. 113).

Migrant Rapitok men who had become elders were in the best position to exploit the new economic opportunities to their own advantage. At the same time they retained their traditional economic obligations to the members of their matrilineage, in particular to the young single men. According to tradition, young men acquired property only after they had married and set up their own household. Single men lived in special young men's houses built with the aid of their elder and other matrilineage members. They often cultivated their own gardens and sometimes even prepared their own food, though usually they ate with their parents or maternal kin. If a young man required any shell money, he approached his elder for a loan and then worked for the latter until he had paid off his debt.

In the traditional system the elder did provide for the needs of the young men of his matrilineage while in return they worked for him and helped him cultivate his gardens. These reciprocal obligations were still continued in Rapitok in 1960, although some of the young men were getting dissatisfied with the system. I witnessed a typical dispute between a young man and his elder. The young man complained that he had planted cocoa on some of his own matrilineage section lands with the agreement of his elder, and then, when the trees were beginning to bear, his elder insisted on pocketing the money from the sale of the wet beans. The elder replied to this accusation that he had clothed the young man for years and given him money on several occasions for pleasure trips to Rabaul. He therefore regarded it as his right to collect the money for the cocoa that the young man had planted.

The case could not be decided by parish elders on the spot but had to be referred to one of the important elders of the matrilineage residing in a nearby parish. It took a whole day of arguments and discussion before a settlement was reached whereby a border was drawn between the trees to which the young man was given usufructuary rights, and those for which the elder retained full rights. A compromise was reached whereby some of the trees planted by the young man were included in the part allocated to the elder. These trees were generally regarded as compensation for the support the elder had given the young man during the previous few years. The latter was not very happy about the compromise but accepted it under pressure from other elders. This dispute and its settlement illustrates two important changes in Tolai economic organisation. First of all, it shows a breaking down of the traditional reciprocal obligations between elders and young men. This breakdown can be expected eventually to undermine the strategic economic position occupied by the matrilineage section elder. This in turn will have far-reaching social and political effects. Secondly, it indicates the germ of the development of a system of individual land-ownership, though this is not yet explicit. However, since cocoa is a perennial crop, the drawing of a border around cocoa land and the vesting of usufructuary rights in the young man pointed to the beginning of vesting full rights of ownership in an individual. Under the settlement, the only limitations to his rights over the cocoa land were the restrictions to selling the land and nominating an heir to it.

European contact initiated economic development and introduced change into what used to be an affluent but static economy. It may be argued that only the most enterprising of Rapitok men had gone to work for Europeans and that therefore their greater capital accumulation was the result of an innate promotion ability rather than of their contact with Europeans, or that only by working for Europeans could they accumulate sufficient cash for investment. This may have been so, but it does not materially alter the fact that European contact encouraged greater entrepreneurship among them and this was marked not only in the accumulation of non-agricultural capital but also in the greater extent to which migrant householders planted cash crops compared with villagers. The distribution of the value of capital assets in sample households (see Table 13) highlights the impact of European contact on Rapitok entrepreneurship. Whereas all migrant elders had capital assets worth more than £1,750, the range among villager elders was from £400 to £1,300 only. Similarly, only 25 per cent of the migrant middle-farmers owned capital assets valued at less than £250, while as many as 43 per cent of villager middle-farmers had assets worth less than that amount. Here we must bear in mind that whereas villager elders held as much as 78 per cent of their total capital assets in the form of tambu, migrant elders had shell money amounting to only one-third of their accumulated capital. This makes the differentiation in terms of productive assets even more striking.

The way European-induced enterprise spread throughout

Table 13

Distribution of value of capital assets in sample households, Rapitok, 1960 (percentages)

£	Migrant elders	Villager elders	Migrant middle-farmers	Villager middle-farmers	Villager single men
0– 250			25	43	100
250– 500		50	50	43	
500– 750			25	14	
750–1,000					
1,000–1,250					
1,250–1,500		50			
1,500 and over	100				
Total	100	100	100	100	100

the population of Rapitok is indicated by the fact that 40 per cent of the 144 households had invested some money in vehicles, 35 per cent in copra driers, 25 per cent in shops, and 10 per cent in sewing machines.* One-third of all those householders who had invested in these capital assets were villagers.

The pattern of capital accumulation among inland Tolai may be seen as one whereby, firstly, the most enterprising young men were attracted to work for Europeans by the availability of a wide variety of goods; secondly, these enterprising men quickly learned to appreciate the advantages of growing cash crops and of investing in capital assets; and thirdly, when they returned home to their own parishes they brought with them these novel ideas for which they soon found a following among villager householders.

A similar pattern emerged in Matupi where as many as 61·3 per cent of young men between the ages of 20 and 29 were urbanites in 1960 (Epstein, A.L., 1963a: 197); that is, migrants, for these young men also had the highest average investment in transport (£144/5/-). Significantly, the next highest investment in the same line was held by a migrant who in his younger days had also worked for Europeans (Epstein,

* These figures are based on the economic census of all Rapitok.

Preparing a coil of tambu

Display of accumulated tambu wealth

Splitting coconuts for copra

Fishing at Matupit

A.L., 1963a: 206). Since data on capital accumulation were collected at a certain moment in time rather than over a period, it is impossible to show the rate of capital growth. Nevertheless, the figures clearly indicate a high propensity to save and invest. The Tolai were mainly interested in imitating expatriate behaviour in the sphere of production.

Yet Nurkse says, with reference to the underdeveloped countries, that the 'small rate of saving is not only due to the low absolute level of real income but also to the high propensity to consume, caused by the allurement of superior forms of consumption' (1962: 67). By contrast, the Tolai appeared to be much more eager to copy European productive activities than European consumption patterns. The prestige attached to ownership of productive assets together with the attraction of a higher standard of living in the future, for which investment provides the means, acted as incentives to entrepreneurs. The demonstration effect operating in the sphere of production brought about an economic differentiation between migrant and villager households. This shows the importance of personal contact by natives with European ventures. Such contact encourages greater efforts in agricultural activities as well as more enterprise in other economic spheres.

Simultaneously with the new stratification, the traditional social standing of elders, middle-farmers and single men households had reasserted itself in the new economic activities. Only those few migrant men who came to occupy the position of matrilineage section elder had managed to acquire considerable amounts of productive assets.

There existed among Rapitok families both a horizontal differentiation between migrant and villager households and a vertical one between elders, middle-farmers and single men households. The vertical differentiation, particularly among migrants, was more marked than the horizontal one, which indicates the resilience of the indigenous social system. In spite of new economic opportunities, the traditional vertical differentiation had persisted. Migrant elders had succeeded in operating the traditional system to their advantage and thereby added to its strength.

5

Subsistence Consumption and Modern Capitalism

In the preceding pages I have shown that in 1960, by virtue of their cash income, the Rapitoks were already fairly well integrated in the wider cash economy. Yet their basic needs of food and shelter were still largely met by subsistence production. They built most of their houses themselves, using native materials. The first two European-type bungalows were in the process of being built for two migrant elders during my stay. More than half the food consumed in the parish consisted of homegrown fruit and vegetables, such as banana, coconut, native spinach, taro or yam.

Pattern of Consumption

Rapitok budget data showed that single men consumed most food per consumption unit; they also spent most on purchased food per month (£2/16/6). This can be easily explained by the fact that they had only themselves to care for, were hungry, and ate a lot. They had no family responsibilities and could therefore afford to spend a large proportion of their cash income, which they derived from working for the local fermentary or from the sale of illicitly brewed liquor, on purchases of food, drink, tobacco and clothes. Only 31 per cent of the value of food consumed per villager elder consumption unit was bought; by contrast migrant elders bought as much as 58 per cent of their food. Similarly, the respective percentages for villager and migrant middle-farmers were 34 per cent and 43 per cent (see Table 14). Imported food, though it may not be

Table 14

Sources of food and sundries consumed per consumption unit in sample households, Rapitok, 1960

	Subsistence[a]								Purchase										Total							
	Food				Sundries				Food				Sundries						Food				Sundries			
													European			Native										
	£	s.	d.	%	£	s.	d.	%	£	s.	d.	%	s.	d.	%	s.	d.	%	£	s.	d.	%	£	s.	d.	%
Migrant:																										
Elder	1	2	1	42		6	3	25	1	9	11	58	15	1	63	2	9	12	2	12	0	100	1	4	1	100
Middle-farmer	1	11	2	57		1	10	25	1	3	0	43	3	10	55	1	4	20	2	14	2	100		7	0	100
Villager:																										
Elder	1	2	5	69			–	–		9	11	31		2	29		9	71	1	12	4	100			11	100
Middle-farmer	1	6	2	66			4	8		13	3	34		9	22	2	11	70	1	19	5	100		4	0	100
Single man	1	7	9	49	1	6	8	79	1	8	9	51	3	3	10	3	9	11	2	16	6	100	1	13	8	100

[a]Evaluation is based on appropriate retail prices in Rabaul.

more nutritious, is certainly more expensive than local produce. Villagers, elders and middle-farmers alike, spent only about two-thirds as much on food as their migrant counterparts. This must not be taken to imply that migrants were better fed than villagers; it simply meant that migrants, having been in European employment and lived away from their home parish at one time or the other, were used to consuming dearer purchased food than were villagers, who had never had any direct European contact.

A similar differentiation was found among coastal Tolai, where those in regular wage employment bought 68 per cent of their food (by value), whereas villagers purchased only 49 per cent (Epstein, A.L., 1963a: 203). However, the range of food items bought by coastal Tolai, in particular urbanites, was much greater than even that of migrant Rapitoks. The latter bought mainly rice, tinned corned beef or mutton, tinned pilchards, some salt, sugar and tea. By contrast

> Tea with sugar but without milk, and bread usually without butter, form today the standard Matupi breakfast . . . the urban worker tends to widen his choice. His regular purchases may include meat from the butchery, butter, tinned vegetables, ketchups and relishes, and his wife uses flour and dripping for cooking (Epstein, A.L., 1963a: 204).

To the Rapitoks a loaf of bread or a tin of milk was still a great and rare luxury; they never bought flour or any type of fat or butter, or any fresh or frozen meat. Local chicken or pigs provided the only sources of fresh meat. Even migrants did not have the direct contact with Rabaul that coastal Tolai, who were employed in the town, had, nor did the former spend as much time in the urban environment as did the latter. This accounted for their limited range of food purchases. Though rice and tinned meat featured prominently, particularly at feasts, all Rapitoks could have quite easily reverted to 100 per cent subsistence food consumption without much hardship.

The same held true for their expenditure on sundries such as tobacco and cigarettes, drinks, areca nuts and lime. Though smoking was widespread, only a small percentage smoked cigarettes. The majority used twist tobacco rolled in newspaper. Moreover, most of the alcoholic drinks and all of the areca nuts and lime consumed were either subsistence produce or bought with tambu rather than cash from other Tolai. Migrants were more committed to cash purchases than were their villager counterparts, also with respect to sundries. 55 per cent of the former's and only 20 per cent of the latter's consumption of sundries was in cash (see Table 14). However, even migrant elders, who were on the whole quite keen smokers, often readily and willingly substituted chewing areca nuts flavoured with lime for smoking tobacco or even cigarettes. Though all expenditure on clothes and household goods was in cash, these two items constituted only a very small part of total consumption. Rapitok families were not really keen on acquiring much non-productive property; most of them still slept on the floor on mats woven out of coconut leaves by their womenfolk; they cooked with hot stones in a hole in the ground, and they ate from leaves, usually with their hands. Migrant householders distinguished themselves from villagers by having a greater number of cooking utensils, plates and cutlery. The only gramophone was owned by a migrant middle-farmer.

Most migrant households had more expensive clothes than did villagers; some migrant men possessed sports coats, which they put on for special occasions. There was very little difference in the clothes worn by womenfolk belonging to migrant and villager households. On working days most women wore only a *laplap*,* and all of them turned up in clean *laplaps* and loose blouses for the Sunday church services. Similarly, men wore only *laplaps* for work—some of them wore European-styled shorts underneath—but they dressed in shorts, shirt and tie on Sundays. Though villagers possessed only half as much of the non-productive property as migrants (see Table 15), there was little difference in the everyday life of migrants and villagers. Except for migrant elders, in whose households total monthly average current expenditure per consumption unit was about £5/10/-, all other established sample households (single men excluded) spent approximately £3/10/- per consumption unit per month. On the whole there was very little differentiation noticeable in the standard of living. Only on Sundays or

* A *laplap* is a cloth about 24 ins. wide and about 2 to 3 yds. long which is wrapped round the waist and tucked in.

Table 15

Average non-productive property of villager and migrant households, Rapitok, 1960

	Villager households												Migrant households							
	Elder				Middle-farmer				Single man				Elder				Middle-farmer			
	£	s.	d.	%	£	s.	d.	%	£	s.	d.	%	£	s.	d.	%	£	s.	d.	%
Clothes	14	0	5	23	11	6	5	35	1	16	0	34	35	16	7	31	13	1	7	23
Luxury goods	28	0	7	46	2	2	7	7		2	7	2	20	2	3	18	17	0	7	30
Household chattels	19	10	5	31	17	17	0	58	3	7	0	64	58	4	2	51	27	5	5	47
Total	61	11	5	100	31	6	0	100	5	5	7	100	114	3	0	100	57	7	7	100

feast days did people dress up. They had thus little wear and tear of their clothes, which accounts for the small amounts currently spent (see Tables 6 and 7).

A large proportion—approximately 75 per cent—of all fares was paid in cash, the remainder in tambu. The charge for return trips to Rabaul ranged from 2/- to 6/-, or between ½ to 1 fathom shell money, depending on the type of vehicle, the number of passengers, and quantity of goods carried. Though each Saturday a majority of Rapitoks travelled to Rabaul market, they spent no more than 5 per cent of their total monthly income on fares (see Tables 6 and 7).

Most gifts received and given were outside the cash sector: they were presentations of either shell money or subsistence food; only rarely was cash given. The pattern of gift receipts and expenditure clearly indicates the considerable degree of social integration which still existed: households were highly interrelated and interdependent. Most transactions were intra-parish. Elders, migrants and villagers alike, gave more than they received: they usually supported some of the young unmarried men of their respective matrilineage section. Young men sometimes treated each other to meals; more frequently, however, they were invited to share their elders' taro or bananas, particularly if they had helped them in cultivating, as they often did. Elders usually organised the bridewealth that had to be given on behalf of the young men belonging to their matrilineage section; they themselves normally contributed a large proportion of the 50 to 100 fathoms tambu which formed part of the customary bridewealth.

In view of their considerable income the Rapitoks might have been expected to spend a large proportion of it on consumption and luxury commodities. Yet everyday life in 1960 was little different from pre-contact times. Though production and income had increased considerably the pattern of wants did not expand in line with growing wealth. The standard of living had in fact not changed much during the last hundred years; it was still almost as described by Parkinson (1887).

Savings: Tambu and Cash

In 1960 traditional thriftiness was still prevalent. This is indicated by current savings as well as by the considerable stock of accumulated cash and shell money. Migrant elders saved 54 per cent of current income and kept 64 per cent of total capital assets in the form of cash and tambu. Villager elders saved 18 per cent of current income and held 84 per cent of capital assets in the shape of cash and shell money. In absolute terms migrant elders had accumulated on average more shell money—2,500 fathoms per household—than villager elders, who had hoarded only 1,300 fathoms per household. In relative terms the shell money hoards represented only 32 per cent of the migrant elders' total capital assets, whereas they represented 78 per cent of the villager elders' capital assets (see Table 8).

The persistence of shell money side by side with cash is one of the striking features of Tolai economic life. In 1960 it was still used as a means of exchange in intra-Tolai trade transactions (see Ch. 7). Whenever adult Rapitok men or women ventured away from home, they carried a small hand-woven bag slung over their shoulders in which they had some small change in shell money. They explained this by saying that, in case they needed to buy some areca nuts or other articles in neighbouring settlements, they wanted to be able to pay for their purchases. Whenever they went as far as Rabaul they carried cash as well as tambu.

The shift of economic power and wealth from the coastal to the inland Tolai brought with it a movement of shell money. Inland Tolai planted taro of which a considerable amount was sold for shell money to coastal Tolai at Rabaul market. By contrast, coastal Tolai had little to offer which other Tolai were prepared to buy. At the same time, the former's traditional prerogative over trips to Nakanai, the source of tambu, had been broken and inland Tolai could now also travel the 200 miles by sea to acquire the appropriate shell. As a result a continuous drift of shell money developed from coastal to inland natives. Rapitok parish as a whole had a net gain of about 600 fathoms in 1960. At a mortuary rite I attended in that year 19 coils of shell money were cut open and distributed. Moreover, the wealth of tambu in inland Tolai settlements enabled the people to hold rites in connection with the male cult of the *tubuan* and *duk duk* more frequently than their coastal neighbours (Epstein, A.L., 1963a: 208). These cults are central in Tolai culture and their persistence is important for the continuation of the traditional social system. The amount of shell money distributed at mortuary rites on the coast was decreasing all the time, yet its importance persisted. In a discussion between young coastal Tolai and their elders during which some young men suggested the abolition of shell money in Tolai society, an elder explained that it provided the skeleton, the bones of the social system; if this is taken away the whole social system will collapse. This was indeed an appropriate analogy. Each contract among Tolai always had been, and still was, confirmed by the passing of shell money. The formation of new social links at a marriage, the dissolution of social ties at a mortuary rite, admission to the *tubuan* society—in fact almost all of the social links between Tolai—were still marked by an exchange of tambu. Some argue that it could be replaced by cash, but cultural values and attitudes cannot be expected to change suddenly—it is for instance difficult to conceive of cash being distributed at mortuary rites—and, more important still, unless the authorities were prepared to exchange it for cash, its abolition would mean the expropriation of all the wealth accumulated by elders. In turn this would bring about their impoverishment and subsequent loss of influence and status. This explains the strong opposition by elders, particularly inland elders, to the abolition of shell money and its replacement by cash. Its abolition would, in fact, amount to a substitution of a new for an old currency without any corresponding compensation being paid for the loss of value of the old currency.

Tolai were generally aware of the different types of goods which could be bought with tambu and with cash: their own produce could be purchased with the former while all European type goods could be bought only with cash. Yet the desire among some Rapitok men to accumulate shell money was so great that they, for instance, charged a few fathoms rather than cash for transporting passengers or goods to Rabaul. They knew full well that the maintenance of their vehicles required cash, but they reckoned that they would use cash derived from the sale of their cocoa or copra to pay for the running of the vehicles while they collected shell money as income from operating their transport enterprises. As a result of this, several disputes were brought before Rapitok's unofficial parish court, because men had accepted shell money in payment for the transport of goods to Rabaul, and then had insufficient cash to pay for the repair of the vehicle when it broke down. On one such occasion, one of the migrant elders, a native local government councillor and a most enterprising man, made a speech, pointing out to his audience the fallacy of mixing the two currencies. He advised his fellow parishioners to go on selling their produce for shell money so as to accumulate hoards—thriftiness in tambu was still a highly desirable thing—but they should accept only cash for goods and services which had to be financed by cash purchases in Rabaul.

If a man wanted to accumulate a lot of shell money at any one time for himself or on behalf of his young son or daughter, he announced that he would hold a *vavalue* function. In preparation he had to plant taro or buy a large quantity of rice; usually he also killed a pig. On the day arranged for the *vavalue,* many people arrived at his hamlet. Each brought between 2 to 10 fathoms of shell money and in turn collected his food parcel. However, this did not mean that the food was being purchased: the amount presented bore no relationship to the quantity of food collected. In fact a careful record was kept of how much each person gave, because subsequently, when the donor himself organised such a *vavalue* it had to be returned. Thus at any one time Tolai had a credit with some and were indebted to others. Many men held functions in the names of their small sons or daughters and many again presented shell money in the name of their small children. Thus children grow up into a network of credits and debts from which they will find it difficult to disentangle themselves as adults. This system of distributing food and collecting shell money enabled a man to accumulate a great deal at one time while saving it over a lengthy period in small amounts. By involving young children in the network of exchanges, Rapitok men attempted to ensure the continuation of shell money as a much desired asset.

In 1960 accumulation of tambu was still one of the main incentives to economic activity, particularly among inland Tolai. Only when a man had accumulated a number of coils could he expect and demand respect from his fellow parishioners. However, there seemed to be an upper limit of about 3,000 fathoms per household beyond which few were interested in accumulating more. In 1960, 3,000 fathoms was regarded as the maximum required for distribution at the mortuary rite after the death of the owner. There was no such concept of an upper limit with regard to cash. This meant that as income per household grew, the rate of shell money accumulation declined while that of cash increased. This is borne out by budget data: migrant elders, who saved most among Rapitok's population, accumulated no more than one-fifth of 1 per cent of their current incomes in this form. By contrast, villager elders, who saved least among the established households, kept as much as 1 per cent of their current income in tambu.

Altogether, savings ratios were considerable; they ranged from 18 per cent of total income including subsistence for villager elders to as much as 54 per cent of total income for migrant elders. The latter, in fact, seemed to save almost all their transport earnings. These high savings ratios illustrate how little Rapitok was as yet integrated into the wider cash economy in terms of everyday expenditure. Moreover, the savings ratios in the budgets are directly related to the total monthly income per consumption unit of the different categories of households. This may be taken as an indication of a diminishing marginal propensity to consume. However, more data collected over a longer period of time are necessary to substantiate this view. Nevertheless, it is obvious that the Rapitoks' everyday consumption in 1960 was largely subsistence orientated. In spite of this they were keen to extend their cash earning capacities. This combination of subsistence living coupled with capitalistic activities no doubt accounts for the rate of Rapitok's economic growth since World War II.

Rapitok Balance of Cash Payments

We have seen that in terms of standard the Rapitoks were still living in a traditional way. Except for the fact that they nowadays wore some clothes, whereas in pre-contact days they covered only their genitals, they conducted their everyday affairs the way they used to do in pre-contact days. There was thus a large element of continuity. Yet, while they continued their traditional activities they were also active in cash cropping and commerce. To show a Tolai parish's involvement in the wider cash economy I calculated Rapitok's balance of cash payments for 1959/60 (see Table 16). Since items of income were not as regular as those of expenditure, I based estimates

Table 16

Estimated balance of cash payments, Rapitok, October 1959-September 1960[a]

Cash Receipts Item	£	%	Cash Expenditure Item	£	%
Crop sales					
Taro[b]	2,400	12	Food[e]	5,695	28
Cocoa (Chinese Traders)[c]	2,150	11	Clothes[e]	372	2
Cocoa (Fermentary)[d]	5,550	29	Sundries[e]	1,595	8
Copra[b]	4,700	23	Feasts (food)[b]	750	4
Miscellaneous[e]	2,550	13	Household chattels[e]	246	1
Wages					
Fermentary[b]	300	2	New Houses[e]	323	2
Miscellaneous[b]	120	–	Vehicle expenses[b]	6,000	31
Transporting[b]	600	3	Council tax[f]	500	2
Trading[b]	240	1	Miscellaneous[e]	550	3
Contracting[b]	250	1	Balance	3,701	19
Miscellaneous[e]	872	5			
Total	19,732	100		19,732	100

[a]This period coincided with the Tolai Cocoa Project's accounting year.

[b]Based on four months' observations (March-June 1960), totals of which were trebled.

[c]Based on four months' observations (March-June 1960) which were taken to represent 40 per cent of annual sales to traders (see p. 125).

[d]Based on Rapitok fermentary records.

[e]Based on sample budgets.

[f]Based on council records.

of most items of income on overall totals I recorded during the four months' period from March to June 1960, whereas items of expenditure are mostly based on budget data. This balance of payments highlights the lack of diversification in the economy. Almost 90 per cent of all cash receipts was derived from crop sales, of which approximately half was contributed by cocoa.

Clearly, cash crops provided the base for participation in the wider economy. The same holds true for the whole of the Territory of Papua and New Guinea: in 1961 cash crops constituted 85 per cent of total produce exported (Fisk, 1966: 34). Rapitok's most important cash crops, cocoa and copra, did not require much effort. Once the ground had been prepared and planted, neither cocoa nor coconuts needed much attention; little weeding was required and this was done by women. Both cocoa and coconut trees are long-lived, yielding crops for many years. Cocoa requires slightly more labour than coconuts. Cocoa trees should be pruned, though the Tolai rarely do this. Cocoa pods have to be picked at the right time, while coconuts are collected only after they have fallen naturally. As cocoa is usually harvested by women, who carry it either to the local fermentary or to their homes, men's labour is restricted to the clearing of bush and planting. The coconut, even more than cocoa, is often termed a 'lazy man's crop', simply because it requires so little male labour. This is reflected in the allocation of time in sample households (see Table 17). For one full week in each of the two sample months I collected data on the time allocation in units of half working days from adult members of the sample households. Table 17 represents the average of the two periods. It clearly illustrates how little effort was involved in cash cropping. Adult males devoted 12 per cent of their working time to clearing bush; they took almost as long over helping their wives in the house and looking after their children. They spent as much time on current cocoa and copra production as they allowed themselves for leisure. 13 per cent of adult male working time was devoted to employment either at the local fermentary or as transport drivers. Young men preferred these jobs to migration. They continued to live at home and were able to combine employment with their own

Table 17

Average allocation of working time in sample households, Rapitok, 1960

	Men %	Women %
Clearing bush	12	–
Garden work: Food	3	20
Cocoa	7	10
Copra	3	7
Employment: Fermentary	10	–
Driver	1	–
Miscellaneous	2	–
Rabaul Trips: Sales	5	3
Purchases	2	–
Housebuilding and repairs	5	–
Housework and child care	11	40
Village meetings	6	2
Church services	10	10
Sickness	5	2
Leisure	10	6
Miscellaneous	8	–
Total	100	100

agricultural activities. Similarly, young South Indian villagers, whose lands had been irrigated, enabling them to grow cash crops, preferred to accept employment on local cane plantations rather than migrate in search of work. They could thus still cultivate their own lands as well as earn a wage on the plantation (Epstein, T.S., 1962: 80). Altogether Rapitok men spent less than half their time on income-earning activities. A similar picture emerges for adult females; they spent 40 per cent of their working time on productive activities. Women did not clear land for cultivation, but they did all the weeding and most of the harvesting. Since much of their subsistence food is highly perishable, they had to go to their gardens almost every other day to collect crops for eating. This accounts for the relatively high proportion of time devoted to food gardens.

Important social and economic consequences follow from

the limited labour requirement of Tolai crops. In the social sphere it enables the people to superimpose innovations such as cash cropping and church attendance on to their traditional way of life. Even the most active Tolai did not necessarily have to break with his traditional obligations. Rapitok's most successful migrant entrepreneur not only found time to organise large feasts, but arranged and participated in traditional dances performed by men. In spite of new and modern pursuits such as controlling large areas of cocoa and coconut gardens as well as operating two trucks, two shops, and a copra drier, he still managed to take an active part in traditional ceremonies and rites. The new economic opportunities, which required large areas of land but little labour, did not offer substitutes but rather supplemented traditional ways. Cash cropping probably did not take up more time than used to be devoted to warfare in pre-contact days. Though the Tolai had always attached great importance to individual enterprise and thrift, part of their competitive spirit used to find expression in fighting. This has now been rechannelled into the economic sphere. Similarly, a tribe of Red Indians, the Kwakiutl, used to fight with weapons, now they fight with property (Codere, 1950: 119).

Participation in the wider economy did not mean that the Tolai had to choose between continuing in the traditional manner or changing to a new pattern—a choice which usually has to be made by labour migrants to urban settlements (Epstein, A.L., 1967). In the Tolai case the new means of earning cash even helped to strengthen certain aspects of their social system rather than undermine it. This is illustrated in the continued importance of tambu, which provides the backbone to Tolai society. The low labour requirement of cash crops helped to perpetuate the traditional social system. At the same time it had important consequences in the economic sphere. It accounted for a low elasticity of supply of cash crops. Though the Tolai were baffled by price fluctuations—they could not grasp the mechanism of international trade—and grumbled when prices fell, they continued to plant more at a steady rate. At the same time they harvested and sold all their surplus crops, almost disregarding the price. Men were inclined to regard income from their cash crops still as windfall profits. This was not surprising considering the rate at which their income grew. My estimates of Rapitok's annual cash receipts for 1950, 1956 and 1959/60 indicate that they more than doubled during the earlier period, while they just about doubled between 1956 and 1959/60. Though my estimates for 1950 and 1956 are probably conservative, on the whole the figures do present a realistic picture. Totals for cocoa yields are the most reliable, since they are largely based on fermentary records. These indicate that cash receipts from the sale of cocoa increased fivefold between 1956 and 1959/60. After World War II Rapitok cultivators concentrated on cocoa, in accordance with the encouragement given by the administration. They hardly extended coconut plantings during this period. This accounts for the fact that copra production had not greatly increased during the latter part of the 1950s.

Since the Tolai contribution to world trade of cocoa and copra is minute, they have no hope of influencing prices by varying the quantities they offer for sale. This probably applies to all the Territory's exports except coffee, which is largely dependent on the limited Australian market, though Australia is not dependent for coffee imports on the comparatively small New Guinea supplies. It can be safely assumed that the Tolai will continue to expand their cash cropping, in spite of possibly falling prices, as long as they have land available for the extension of cultivation. Unless the fall of cocoa and copra prices offsets increasing sales, we can expect Rapitok's cash receipts to continue to grow; if prices remain at their 1959/60 level, they will probably grow at a steady rate of about 15 per cent per year. Therefore prices would have to fall substantially to absorb this considerable rate of growth, which ensures a doubling of cash receipts within five to six years. With a tendency to save more as incomes increase, the higher amount will result in greater savings. In 1959/60 almost one fifth of the total remained unused. Part of this balance found its way into bank savings accounts, the remainder was simply hoarded. Bank deposits represent direct sources of finance. Similarly, hoarded cash—that is unused titles to material resources or services—provides indirect loans to the financial authorities.

A small parish retail store

Hot air copra drier

Rapitok men repairing a jeep

Sellers at Rabaul market

Both from an economic as well as from a general social point of view it would be advantageous for indigenes if they were enabled to invest their funds directly in business enterprises or investment trusts. The concept of owning a small share of a large property is familiar to the Tolai. Their traditional system of landholding was based on this very idea. Three Rapitok migrant elders did in fact approach me with the request that I help them acquire shares in Burns Philp, one of the few large Australian trading firms operating in Rabaul. One of these migrant elders bought, through the Bank of New South Wales, £150 shares in an Australian investment trust. These indigenous capitalists were aware of the possibility of investing their savings productively. Their business acumen was surprising, particularly in view of their lack of schooling. Rapitok's most successful businessman was illiterate. Some commercial training in formal schools, as well as in adult education classes conducted in parishes, would certainly have been welcomed by the people in Rapitok and many other places. Such education might act as an incentive to productive activities in a similar way as did European employment during the inter-war period. At the same time closer contact with expatriate life may stimulate wants for such things as clothing and household chattels.

In 1959/60 Rapitok cash purchases of consumer goods were largely confined to food; one-third of total cash receipts was in fact spent on food. Yet it must be remembered that bought food provided a welcome, but by no means essential, addition. Consequently, the demand of the inland Tolai for bought food was much more elastic than that of the expatriate population.

Investment outside agriculture was largely confined to transport. At least until 1960 trucks and jeeps were the only really large capital assets directly acquired. Though vehicles provided a considerable proportion of migrant elders' income—motor transport can be reasonably profitable enterprise — Rapitok as a whole spent on vehicles as much as one-third of its total annual cash receipts. The transport did carry some loads for neighbouring parishes, but the great majority of traffic came from residents. All this shows that the various trucks and jeeps met an important internal need in the parish. Except for the cocoa sold to the local fermentary, all other cash crops had to be transported to the buying centres. The numerous vehicles, therefore, represented capital assets which were essential for transporting produce to the markets. Vehicle expenses amounted to about half the gross receipts from crops sold outside Rapitok—crop sales less cocoa sold to the fermentary (see Table 16). The cost of transport was considerable. However, the alternative to acquiring and running their own transport would have been to hire European- or Chinese-owned trucks in Rabaul. This arrangement would in fact have been more expensive in the long run, apart from necessitating a more formal selling organisation among growers; moreover, sellers would have had difficulty in returning to their parish, since the hired trucks were based in Rabaul, whereas their own trucks always had to make the return journey.

Vehicles constituted a profitable investment for individual owners as well as a considerable source of prestige. During my stay a migrant elder tried to get one of the big oil companies operating in Rabaul to install a petrol pump in his hamlet. Being a capable mechanic, he intended setting up a service station to cater for maintenance and repair of all vehicles in the vicinity. Many Rapitok migrants, and even some villagers, behaved very much like modern capitalists. A number of them employed labourers to help them in their agricultural as well as commercial enterprises. These labourers either originated from the neighbouring Bainings or were plantation workers from the mainland who had broken their contracts. In either case, the labourers were prepared to work for a pitiful wage. Their employers, like typical capitalists, were chiefly interested in making profits and exploited their cheap labour.

Industrial Development and Intra-Tolai Finance

The quite considerable savings ratio among Rapitok people clearly indicates that their economic development was not a problem of credits (Shand, 1966: 100), but rather one of channelling savings into profitable and productive enterprises. In order to help the indigenous population in starting and operating profit-making businesses, the administration began in 1964 to offer a business advisory service in Rabaul. Though the advisory staff have gone out amongst the people in their attempt to have frank talks with budding Tolai entrepreneurs, it would appear that they have not managed, as yet, to gain the confidence and trust of the population. This may be due to the fact that the officials are associated with the administration and the shrewd Tolai suspect that if they disclosed their financial resources and openly discussed their economic potentials, tax demands might follow. According to a statement made by the business advisory officer, Rabaul (dated 17 Feb. 1967), the advisory activities were mainly connected with transport and retail enterprises. The Tolai were still keen on expanding their investment in trucks and stores, in spite of the many inefficient and unprofitable enterprises which already existed. This clearly indicates that their economic horizon was still largely limited to service industries which by their very nature were protected from foreign competition.

The advisory staff tried to encourage the purchase of shares in Territory companies, yet the people did not show themselves keen to follow this advice, except in the case of Palnamadaka Co. Ltd. This company was formed to take over an expatriate furniture manufacturing business situated in the vicinity of Rabaul. The firm was bought at the beginning of 1966 for a total of £25,000, 40 per cent of which was raised by means of 10,000 individual £1 shares, 36 per cent was lent by the expatriate initiators of the business, and the remaining 24 per cent originated from a Commonwealth Bank loan. The board of directors and all shareholders are indigenes, most of them Tolai. Practically all shareholders came from the coastal areas of the Gazelle Peninsula; virtually no capital was contributed by any inland people. One of the original owners of the firm has been retained as a salaried manager. Palnamadaka Co. Ltd appears to have done remarkably well: it was hoped to declare a 10 per cent dividend at the end of its first financial year of operation. Unfortunately no data are available on the way Tolai were induced or attracted to buy shares. It would be interesting to know about kin and friendship ties among shareholders and so on.*

By 1966, the Paparatava Development Co. Ltd, a Catholic

* I intend to investigate the formation and operation of Palnamadaka Co. Ltd on my next visit to the Gazelle Peninsula.

mission-sponsored timber enterprise, was the second of the only two companies in which Tolai capital predominated. There were certain signs that the Tolai wanted to diversify their economic activities. Yet external trade is bound to remain dominated by agriculture for many years to come. Diversification of economic activities may take place in agriculture or import substitution, but hardly as an attempt to export manufactured articles.

Tolai customary thriftiness stood them in good stead in the sphere of cash savings; their traditional social network of kin and friendship ties, on the other hand, tended to impede intra-Tolai loans. For instance, according to the business advisory officer (communication dated 17 Feb. 1967), a Rapitok man required £100 to complete a piggery. This seemed a sound enterprise and had been supervised by the Department of Agriculture. As an experiment the service approached the owner of a successful Rabuana trucking and trade store business, which had been assisted by the service. This businessman had surplus funds and was offered up to 10 per cent interest on a loan of £100 for one year, yet he was not prepared even to consider a loan for the venture. The advisory officer believed that this was due to tribal jealousy. On the contrary, I would suggest the reason for this apparently irrational behaviour was a fear, justified by experience, that pressures emanating from kin and friendship ties would prevent the lawful settlement of the debt. Though there may have been no immediate link between the businessman and the entrepreneur, the former was probably afraid that the latter might try to pull strings through the chain relationship which ultimately links all Tolai, so as to avoid repayment of the loan, let alone interest payment. The widespread social network tended to impede intra-Tolai finance of enterprises and consequently slowed down their rate of economic expansion.

Economic Change and Traditional Society

In pre-contact days the Tolai father's kin-group's responsibility for his sons was recognised by making it obligatory for the former to provide land for subsistence cultivation by the latter. Plots thus granted were used for two or three years, after which the land was allowed to revert to bush fallow. Therefore, the temporary provision of plots for subsistence cultivation did not in any way imply that the land was permanently transferred from one descent group to another: in fact it remained vested in the donor's group.

The introduction of perennial cash crops complicated the pattern of land use and created strains and stresses. Many Rapitok cash croppers wanted their sons, who had helped in the establishment and maintenance of their gardens, to be entitled to inherit their agricultural property, rather than their nearest male uterine relative, who more often than not resided in a different parish and who had never lifted a finger to help in the cultivation of the gardens. Yet this desire contradicts the traditional system of matrilineal inheritance. In order to forestall difficulties which might arise after their deaths, some men planted cocoa on their own matrilineage lands, yet did so in the name of their young sons and with their active support and help. In this way as much as 18 per cent of the surveyed gardens was planted for and by sons of men belonging to matrilineage section H (see Map IV). One-third of this squatter cultivation was cocoa and the remainder coconuts and bananas. Altogether of Rapitok's 66,000 cocoa trees, only 40,000 (62 per cent) were cultivated on the appropriate matrilineal lands, 6,000 (9 per cent) were planted on lands which had been bought outright, 1,000 trees were on lands belonging to the grower's wife's matrilineage and 19,000 trees (28 per cent) were on lands which were vested in the grower's father's kin-group. When I inquired from some of the fathers concerned what they visualised would happen to claims to these gardens after their own death, they explained that their sons were not only keen cultivators, but they were also thrifty in the accumulation of tambu, which should enable them to inherit at least some of their fathers' landed wealth.

Tolai custom lays down that a man can stake a claim to property belonging to an elder by distributing shell money at his mortuary rite. In theory this tradition applied to any one, in practice it was usually limited to near kin of the deceased; it had always enabled sons to claim at least part of their father's property after his death. This custom provided the basis for some Rapitok fathers' expectations that, when they died, their own sons would be able to inherit the gardens, which had been planted on their matrilineage lands, rather than on that of their sons, simply by bringing coils of shell money to the mortuary rite and distributing it to all present.

Most of the Rapitok men who had developed cash cropping were still alive in 1961; it is therefore difficult to predict what will happen to their perennial tree crops when the present generation dies. Before I left Rapitok in 1961 only one migrant elder with large cocoa and coconut gardens had died. At the mortuary rite held in his honour, his two sons lavishly cut up their coils of tambu and distributed great quantities among all guests. In return they claimed about one half of their father's gardens. The dead man's classificatory sister's eldest son, his rightful heir, was less generous in his tambu distribution. He was himself an older man, who had planted a large area with cocoa and coconuts and was not so keen on inheriting the total garden lands, and therefore did not even try to contest the sons' claims, which were backed by public opinion expressed at the mortuary rite. Subsequently the elders praised the generosity displayed by the sons in distributing so much tambu; they criticised the rightful heir for his stinginess.

The considerable area of virgin bush which was still available for cultivation in 1961 (see p. 77) clearly indicated that there was as yet no real pressure of population on land, in spite of extensive cash cropping. However, there was already some competition for centrally situated lands. Most inhabitants preferred to live along the roadside, while the virgin bush was some distance from their homes. This led to competition for conveniently placed lands and often resulted in quarrels, not only between individuals, but also between whole kin-groups. These disputes were frequently responsible for serious losses in terms of productive assets. All this clearly emerges from the following dispute.

An area of about 5 acres, situated along the roadside, bordering hamlet 31 (see Map III) had been planted with coconuts and cocoa by To Molom with aid from members of his kin-group. To Molom, who had been a 'big man' in the area, died in 1956 and To Leima, his classificatory younger brother, who took over his property, in turn died in 1959. Tarai, who at that time was probably the most respected and important villager elder in Rapitok, claimed that a large part of this land (about $3\frac{1}{2}$ acres) actually belonged to his descent-group, rather than to To Molom's. According to Tarai he had reminded To Molom when he first saw the latter clear it pre-war, that the land in question belonged mainly to Tarai's and partly (about 1 acre) to the matrilineage section of another elder, Turme. However, at first To Molom planted only subsistence crops on the lands and according to Tarai he promised to pay rent in tambu (*totokom*) for the usufructuary right on the land. In fact this was never paid. When To Leima inherited To Molom's gardens Turme reminded him that part of the land was vested in his own matrilineage, whereupon To Leima offered to buy it for 5 fathoms tambu, but the purchase never took place. Then on To Leima's death Tarai and Turme decided to distribute 5 fathoms tambu each, announcing to all present at the mortuary rite that they were doing this in order to reward To Leima's kin-group for the cocoa and coconut trees on the disputed land and that they now wanted to reclaim it for themselves. However, Talia, To Leima's classificatory sister's son, was not prepared to accept this arrangement: a few days after the mortuary rite he and Tenanil, another member of his matrilineage, who was from Napapar, a neighbouring parish, and who had come to Rapitok after World War II at the invitation of To Molom, returned the 10 fathoms to Tarai and Turme, saying that they had no intention of giving up the land concerned; to the best of their knowledge it was their own. If Tarai and Turme, being elders, claimed to own the land, then Talia and Tenanil wished to buy it. Tarai, however, was not prepared to discuss a possible sale of the land and decided to take the dispute to the unofficial village court, where, as the most respected villager elder, he had hopes of being able to settle the case to his satisfaction.

At the hearing, which I attended early in 1960, Talia angrily said to Tarai, 'It is easy for you to do as you like here in Rapitok these days, because you are the only knowledgeable old man around the place, but beware, if you cheat us young people of our rights and our lands, you will be judged in your next life'. Since Tarai pursued a completely uncompromising attitude,

Talia, Tenanil and some other members of their matrilineage left the meeting in a huff and went off to the land under dispute where, in great anger, they chopped down all the coconut and cocoa trees, which by then were already in full bearing. When Tarai was told of their action he said that he did not mind, since all he was interested in was to get the land back under his control. Nevertheless, the case came before the local patrol officer, who seemed to be upset by Tarai's conceited attitude for he said, 'You elders, you think because you are old you can claim any piece of land on which you set your eyes. You see that there is no old man in another matrilineage and so you start claiming that kin-group's land as your own. I will not let you elders get away with this'. Since he could not decide ownership of land—this is a matter for the native land commissioner—he ruled 'that the land under dispute may be used by Talia until such date as the native land commissioner reaches another decision. Until then my word is law'. Tarai, however, did not leave the matter at that. He took it up with the native land commissioner, who after lengthy negotiations laid down the tri-partite division of the area concerned: about 2½ acres went to Tarai, 1½ to Talia and 1 acre to Turme. In the meantime, the whole area had reverted to bush since the trees had been cut down. Moreover, members of Tarai's kin-group were not on speaking terms with Talia's descent group, nor did the former patronise Tenanil's village store.

This case shows clearly a number of important aspects of modern life in Rapitok, in particular the continued strategic importance of *lualuas,* traditional elders, who supported their power and influence by their extensive knowledge of customary claims to land. Hardly any member of their society dared to question their superior understanding of the age-old landholding pattern. This meant that younger men had to seek support for their land claims from external sources, such as the administration, in opposition to their own elders. Moreover, we see the disadvantageous economic implications of the traditional landholding pattern as well as the disruption in social relations which it causes. However, as long as demand for land in Rapitok does not reach the limit of cultivable soils it is unlikely that disputes will feature greatly in intra-parish social interaction.

In some coastal settlements where the shortage of land, accentuated by land alienation, had already become crucial by 1960, land disputes were frequent and often insoluble (Epstein, A.L., 1963a: 212). Though Rapitok was still one of the most fortunate settlements with respect to the availability of land, even there the population had begun to be aware of pressures. Cultivators reduced the period of fallow: it used to be seven to ten years and was in 1960 only four to six years. Elders decided to reserve an area of bush land of approximately 150 acres for subsistence; on this land no one was allowed to plant perennial cash crops. If 1960 trends of population increase (Epstein and Epstein, 1962: 80) and extension of cash crops continue at present rates, by 1975 almost all Rapitok land will be either under cultivation with food or perennial cash crops, or in temporary fallow but destined for the growing of subsistence crops. As soon as the margin of available cultivable lands is approached, we can expect several consequences. First and foremost, serious quarrels will arise over claims to lands, which may disrupt the whole parish society. Secondly, the elasticity of supply of cash crops will most likely increase, that is a slight fall in cocoa prices might induce growers to neglect their cocoa trees, or even to chop some down in order to make room for some more remunerative crop or necessary subsistence cultivation. Since perennial cash crops usually involve long-term investment of land and labour, such changing of crops may prove to be disastrous.

The problem of claims to land is made even more complex by the inconsistencies which arise because the system of matrilineal inheritance is associated with patri-virilocal residence. Problems of inheritance and succession are not new; they are at least as old as experience of European contact. Pullen-Burry reported at the beginning of this century that the wife of a New Zealand planter had been asked by Tolai natives to give her advice in a dispute which had arisen concerning some property. The question at issue was whether the white man's way of inheritance from father to son was to be adopted or whether the ancient way from uncle to nephew was to be retained. Subsequently, she heard that after lengthy discussion they had decided that the European code was preferable to their own in this instance (1909: 225). Unfortunately we lack details of the case in question; yet it highlights the flexibility in the customary social system. An exception to the rules was readily made in order to meet the requirements of a particular case, while at the same time the traditional system continued practically unchanged. The case mentioned had not set a precedent for rulings in subsequent disputes. The problem of inheritance and succession in a matrilineal society is still looming large on the Tolai horizon.

The existence of large capital assets adds a further difficulty to the persistence of the customary system of matrilineal inheritance. By 1960 Rapitok men had not yet had to face up to this, but they were showing signs of awareness of its existence. One migrant elder truck owner and one migrant middle-farmer had registered their vehicles in the names of their young sons. When their fathers die, the sons will be legal and rightful owners of the vehicles. Such a solution to the problem was possible only in the rarer instances of sole ownership of assets. It could not be applied when assets were jointly owned by members of a descent group. Yet in a number of cases the son of the elder in control of the vehicle helped his father and frequently also acted as driver and looked after it. However, according to custom and law the vehicle belonged to his father's kin-group and on the death of the elder his son will have no rightful claim to the vehicle at all; the elder's share, as well as his right of control over the vehicle, will have to be passed on to his sister's son, who probably lived in another parish and had never had anything at all to do with the running of the vehicle. The existence of costly and indivisible capital assets further heightened the tensions not only between sons and sister's sons but also between the respective descent-groups involved.

In this chapter I have tried to show how favourable conditions enabled the Rapitoks in particular and the Tolai in general to superimpose cash earning activities on to their traditional way of life: they could continue their subsistence living and simultaneously produce cash crops as well as develop capitalistic service industries. However, they were fast approaching a critical stage in many aspects of their economic and social life: population growth coupled with extensive and perennial cash cropping was responsible for a growing land shortage; prospects of diversifying their economy were poor and investment outlets accordingly restricted; the expansion of secondary as well as tertiary industries was limited by the small size of the market. In turn all this was reflected in strains and stresses in the general social and political sphere: the new economic opportunities which had resulted in a growing land shortage were responsible for undermining the pivotal position of traditional elders; matrilineal descent and inheritance were beginning to be threatened. In spite of all this, the customary social system was still predominant. Its persistence was in fact adversely affecting economic development.

6

Cocoa Production and Sales

Cocoa reached the Territory via Samoa from Ceylon. It was introduced to the Gazelle Peninsula by German planters at the beginning of this century. Some of the indigenous population did begin to grow a little cocoa in the inter-war period, but most of the trees were lost through neglect, or damage during World War II. For some years after 1945, most Tolai were preoccupied with re-establishing their homesteads, subsistence gardens, and coconut groves. Nevertheless they watched with keen interest the rapid expansion of non-native cocoa plantings. By 1951 there must have been at least 255,000 cocoa trees on foreign-owned plantations on New Britain (see Table 18).* This induced some Tolai to experiment with cocoa. They were encouraged by the Australian administration, who had first established that the crop was well suited to local conditions of soil and climate. The administration was fully aware at the time of the many difficulties involved in establishing a native cocoa industry. 'Accordingly, in 1951 the Departments of Agriculture and Native Affairs combined in a vigorous extension campaign designed to systemise the infant Tolai cocoa industry while it was still feasible to do so' (Department of the Administrator, 1965: 1).

In order to prevent the haphazard planting of cocoa trees through bush areas and to facilitate disease control, an ordinance was introduced in 1952 to regulate the growing of cocoa. According to this ordinance, 'A person shall not plant or keep planted cocoa trees unless he is registered or provisionally

* Based on total output (*Annual Report,* 1959) divided by average tree productivity (2·2 lb.).

Table 18

Non-indigenous cocoa trees and cocoa production (New Britain)

Year ending 31 March	Immature trees (000)	Mature trees (000)	Production (dry lb.)	Average dry beans per mature tree (lb.)
1951	?	255[a]	561,680[b]	2·2[a]
1959[c]	2,834	1,638	3,625,824	2·2
1960[c]	2,874	2,096	4,862,055	2·3
1961[c]	3,677	2,726	5,835,378	2·1
1962[c]	4,314	3,414	8,256,501	2·4
1963[c]	4,350	4,301	11,740,288	2·7
1964[c]	4,031	5,046	12,474,224	2·4
1965[c]	3,841	5,866	16,325,792	2·7

[a]Estimate based on total output divided by 2.2 lb., *i.e.*, average production per tree in 1959.

[b]New Guinea *Annual Report* 1950/51.

[c]*Production Bulletins*, Part I, Rural Industries (1959-65).

registered as a cocoa grower; penalty Fifty pounds'. Moreover, 'A person is not eligible for registration as a cocoa grower unless he owns, leases or manages an area of land on which there are not less than five hundred cocoa trees in continuous grove, planted as prescribed' (T.P.N.G., 1952: 2). The Tolai readily followed the lead and advice given them by administrative officials. 'In 1954/5 an agricultural survey of cocoa listed 487,174 trees registered under the Cocoa Ordinance, and 697,285 additional trees reported. This gave a total for the area of the five (Tolai) Native Local Government Councils of 1,184,459 trees in all stages of development' (Williamson, 1958: 595). Within only a few years the number of cocoa trees planted by the Tolai reached a figure equivalent to 35 trees per head. Their cocoa plantings more than doubled in the subsequent five years. The Department of Agriculture estimated that by 1960 a total population of 40,000 had 2,941,000 cocoa trees—a per capita holding of 74. No attempt was made at the time to estimate how many of these cocoa trees were already in full bearing. However, this percentage

Table 19

Tolai dry bean cocoa production and cocoa trees

Year ending 31 December	Tolai Cocoa Project[a] lb.	%	Traders lb.	%	Total lb.	%	Percentage change	Mature trees	Registered cocoa trees
1953	38,752	50[b]	38,748[b]	50[b]	77,500	100		35,200[e]	
1954	136,476	55[b]	111,824[b]	45[b]	248,100	100	+ 220	112,700[e]	
1955	373,408	60[b]	248,892[b]	40[b]	622,300	100	+ 150	282,800[e]	1,184,459[g]
1956	807,744	65[b]	434,856[b]	35[b]	1,242,600	100	+ 100	564,800[e]	
1957	1,376,928	70[b]	590,072[b]	30[b]	1,967,000	100	+ 57	894,000[e]	
1958	1,580,668	70[b]	677,332[b]	30[b]	2,258,000	100	+ 14	1,027,000[e]	
1959	2,053,632	60[c]	1,369,088[c]	40[c]	3,422,700	100	+ 50	1,555,700[e]	
1960	2,253,664	60[c]	1,502,436[d]	40[c]	3,756,100	100	+ 10	1,705,000[e]	2,940,955[h]
1961	2,825,088	60[c]	1,881,312[d]	40[c]	4,706,400	100	+ 25	2,139,200[e]	3,096,674[h]
1962	3,728,032	59[c]	2,590,668[d]	41[c]	6,318,700	100	+ 34	2,872,100[e]	3,422,656[h]
1963	4,010,048	52[c]	3,701,552[d]	48[c]	7,711,600	100	+ 20	3,505,200[e]	3,471,129[h]
1964	3,418,912	46[c]	4,013,488[d]	54[c]	7,432,400	100	— 5	3,716,200[f]	3,557,258[h]
1965	3,359,552	36[c]	5,972,448[d]	64[c]	9,332,000	100	+ 20	4,241,800[e]	3,623,058[h]

[a]Figures supplied by Tolai Cocoa Project.

[b]Estimate only (see p. 121).

[c]Report from Cocoa Inspector, Rabaul.

[d]Calculated total based on Tolai Cocoa Project and cocoa inspection figures.

[e]Calculated totals based on total Tolai cocoa production divided by 2·2 lb., the average dry bean yield per tree.

[f]Climatic difficulties in 1964 reduced cocoa yields to an estimated 2 lb. per tree (see Table 22).

[g]Williamson, 1958: 595.

[h]Department of Agriculture, Rabaul, communication dated 17 Oct. 1966.

can be roughly calculated by examining the total quantity of dry cocoa produced by growers in that year (see Table 19) and dividing it by 2·2 lb. (the average yield of dry cocoa per mature tree). This calculation shows that by 1960 more than 50 per cent of all the trees were already bearing. In the same year there were 4,970,000 non-indigenous cocoa trees on New Britain of which 43 per cent were already fully matured (see Table 22).

Cocoa production increased rapidly; a great number of cultivators grew trees on small holdings and consequently the individual producer had very little bargaining strength in the market. Unless steps were taken to organise the native industry so that it had efficient processing and marketing procedures, there was the danger that it might become chaotic. which in turn might have had adverse effects on the overall development of the Territory's cocoa industry. Therefore, the administration was concerned that native growers should produce a uniformly high quality cocoa which could be sold on the world market at a satisfactory price.

Concomitant with the growing cocoa industry was the development of the native local government councils. In 1950 the Tolai were selected as the chief testing ground for the new area council policy. The first two local government units were established in 1950, and by 1953 most of the area was administered through five councils. Subsequent amalgamations reduced the number to four and in 1964 these merged into one single council—the Gazelle Peninsula Local Government Council.

Tolai Cocoa Project

The new councils, which were empowered to levy rates and taxes, were keen to sponsor local economic development so as to help provide increasing prosperity. At that time it was already clear that centrally controlled fermentaries were needed to make the cocoa enterprise a success. These two factors combined brought about the union between the new cocoa industry and the new councils in the form of the Tolai Cocoa Project, which developed in three phases.

First phase: In 1951, after a series of meetings between the councils, leading growers, and officers of the Departments of Agriculture and Native Affairs, it was decided that initially each council would appropriate funds from its revenue to construct fermentary units at strategic places in their areas and would further provide recoverable advances to enable each fermentary to start operating. Furthermore, special courses for selected trainee fermentary clerks were arranged at the Vunadadir Local Government Centre, and a simple accounting procedure, geared to the limitations of the clerks, was designed. The first council grant was made in 1951, when the Vunamami Native Local Government Council appropriated from its revenue £240 for the construction of a cocoa fermentary at Ngatur. An additional £64 was allocated to provide sun drying facilities. In 1953 the Reimber/Livuan Council followed the Vunamami example and built its first cocoa processing centre at Pelegir. Each fermentary was set up to operate as a financial entity separate from its parent council. There was no capital subscription from growers. Each grower who wished to have his wet beans processed and sold, registered with one of the fermentaries, which paid advances on wet bean intake and a final settlement after the consignment had been sold and operating costs deducted. Cocoa was marketed under the name of the individual fermentaries: at no stage in its operation did the relevant fermentary or parent council assume ownership of the produce.

> Prior to organizing the second (bank finance) phase of the Project, the feasibility of handling the industry through orthodox co-operative techniques was examined and rejected. By 1951 the Co-operative Movement in the Tolai area, concerned with copra marketing and retailing, had fallen into serious financial difficulties and no longer commanded popular support . . . Even had the growers been agreeable, private enterprise was not interested in providing the necessary facilities, and, in fact, was most sceptical regarding the chances of any large-scale native scheme being successful. Moreover, European plantation owners in the area were at the time preoccupied with the rehabilitation and expansion of their own holdings (Department of the Administrator, 1965: 3).

Second phase: Cocoa production increased rapidly in the

early 1950s, and more fermenting facilities were urgently required. Considerable capital investment, beyond the revenue resources of the councils, was needed. Accordingly, the councils concerned applied to the administration for financial assistance. In 1954 the Reimber/Livuan Council was granted a £1,000 loan at $4\frac{3}{4}$ per cent from the administration treasury, repayable at the rate of £500 per year. Vunamami and Vundadir councils each received £2,000 on similar terms. The loaned money was spent partly on the establishment of new cocoa processing centres and partly on the extension of already existing fermentaries. Moreover, the Reimber/Livuan Council obtained a non-interest bearing loan of £1,310 from the Department of Agriculture to construct a specially designed concrete hot air dryer. Additional finance for capital equipment amounting to £9,021 was forthcoming from the growers themselves: they agreed to invest the undistributed final settlements of several consignments of cocoa that had been sold.

Third phase: Even the expanded fermenting capacity proved unable to cope with the rapidly growing production. Consequently, in 1955 officers of the Departments of Native Affairs and of Agriculture set about carefully examining the whole cocoa industry, including a count of all native cocoa trees and an estimate of future wet bean production. The census showed that 1,184,459 trees had been planted. Accurate calculation of the total production to be expected in subsequent years was impeded by the lack of knowledge regarding the average yield per tree over the area, and the probable survival rate of cocoa trees. Some experimental blocks at Kerawat Agricultural Experimental Station were at that time yielding 7 lb. of dried beans per tree annually, with the yield still rising. Though the immediate fermenting capacity required was finally calculated on an estimated yield of 4 lb. of dried beans per tree, it soon became apparent that even that estimate was too optimistic: the average yield of dry beans per cocoa tree in bearing turned out to be no more than 2·2 lb. This in fact coincides closely with productivity on non-indigenous plantations in New Britain as a whole (see Table 18).

Final estimates of fermenting installations required in 1955, taking into consideration the flush periods under Gazelle

Peninsula climatic conditions, laid down a need for twelve processing centres involving a cost of approximately £80,000. After long discussions between growers and administrative officials concerned, the Bank of New South Wales agreed to make loans to the councils up to this amount at 4¾ per cent interest per annum. The administration guaranteed the loans, provided each council pledged its assets as security for the period of the loan. Since the first loan in 1956, loan funds made available to the councils have increased to £277,000. Repayment of the loans had initially been fixed by way of deduction of £35 per ton of dried cocoa produced. Subsequently the deduction has been progressively reduced so that in 1966 it was no more than £10 per ton of dried cocoa beans. Almost 75 per cent of the initial loans had been repaid by 31 March 1966.

The Tolai Cocoa Project grew rapidly. In 1953 its first two fermentaries had an annual output of about 17 tons dried cocoa beans. By 1965 it had eighteen fermentaries with an annual output of 1,510 tons dry cocoa. The project is run on a non-profit basis. It has no formal constitution and is not itself a corporate body. Legally, all the project's assets were originally vested in the five councils, which were responsible for organising and financing the scheme. Since the amalgamation of these units in 1964 (see p. 117), all project assets have become vested in the Gazelle Peninsula Native Local Government Council. In February 1958 it had been agreed with the councils that the project's board of management should handle all matters relating to the project other than the raising of any additional finance that might be required. In 1965 the board was composed of the deputy district commissioner (New Britain), who acted as chairman, the executive officer of the Tolai Cocoa Project, an official of the Department of Agriculture, the district agricultural officer (East New Britain), representatives (elected by the growers) from each of the eighteen fermentaries, and four councillors (appointed by the Gazelle Peninsula Local Government Council). The administration still subsidised the project by paying the salaries of the executive officer, the technical agricultural field officer, and the accounts officer. All other staff employed by the project was paid out of project funds. Tolai by far outnumbered European members on the project's board. Thus, in theory at least, control over the board could have been exercised by Tolai themselves. However, since none of them had as yet sufficient business training and managerial ability, they usually followed the advice and guidance given by European administrative officers.

The Drift away from the Project

In spite of its obvious usefulness, the project has had to face serious competition from European and Chinese traders ever since its inception. In order to protect their enterprise the local government councils ruled that it was illegal for any Tolai to sell cocoa outside the project. A number of Tolai were actually fined for offences under this rule. However, the Department of Crown Law in Port Moresby decided that this piece of council legislation was *ultra vires* and to the great regret of many leading Tolai the rule had to be dropped. Since then there has been a clamouring for protective legislation. At almost every meeting of the project's board of management complaints were raised by Tolai members themselves about cocoa sales to independent traders. At the 29th meeting of the board held on 4 January 1961 a motion was proposed by a leading Tolai and passed by a large majority that the 'Minister be requested to bring in legislation to compel all Tolai people within council areas to take their wet beans to council fermentaries'. The board aimed at full monopsony over all Tolai cocoa. However, the administration, in accordance with its policy of encouraging competitive enterprise in the Territory, has not thought such protective legislation desirable or justifiable.

The drift away from the project has taken on considerable proportions. The cocoa inspector's reports, available only from 1959 onwards, indicate that the percentage of cocoa handled by the project declined from 60 per cent in 1959 to 36 per cent in 1965. I estimate that in 1953, when the project had only two fermentaries, it handled only half the Tolai cocoa output. As the number of fermentaries increased, the project processed a greater proportion, reaching a maximum of 70 per cent in 1958, from which period onwards the proportion declines markedly (see Table 19). Since 1959 the percentage of cocoa sold to the project appears to be inversely related to the quantities of wet beans produced; that is, as production increases a greater proportion is sold to independent traders. The *South Pacific Post* of 8 July 1960 carried an article headed 'Chinese Taking Cocoa Trade', according to which an administration official in Rabaul held that the

> Chinese fermentary owners were 'milking' cocoa from the Tolai cocoa project with offers of immediate cash payment. He said that the drift away from the native fermentaries was 'sizeable'. It was first thought there were two main reasons for the success of the independent fermentaries, the spokesman said. They were a possible illegal liquor outlet for the natives and a 'no questions asked' depot for disposing of stolen cocoa. But it now appeared that there was no definite single reason for the native growers to turn to the independent Chinese fermentaries. On paper the project position 'looked good'. The fermentaries were processing greater quantities each year. But this was due to the rise in grower production — the Chinese were also taking more and more of the total percentage basis.

In 1963 the ban on native consumption of alcohol was lifted. According to some opinions, this should have removed the major incentive for Tolai to sell their cocoa to Chinese traders. Yet the drift away from the project continued to increase. The project's activities appear to have declined not only in relative, but also in absolute terms. The total dry bean output by the project increased until 1963 when it reached a peak of 4,010,048 lb.; it fell to 3,418,912 lb. in 1964 and dropped further to 3,359,552 lb. in 1965. The decline in the project's processing activities in 1964 can be explained by climatic conditions which adversely affected the cocoa crop in that year. Total output increased again by about 20 per cent in 1965, but the project handled less cocoa in that year than in the previous one (see Table 19).

A number of reasons are frequently advanced to account for the project's decreasing popularity. Some hold that Chinese traders nowadays offer illicit methylated spirit to Tolai who are attracted by this and consequently take their wet beans to traders rather than to the project. Though this may be so in a number of cases, it cannot possibly account for the whole of cocoa sales to independent traders; nor can there be regular thefts of such large quantities that stolen cocoa can provide a major source of cocoa sold outside the project.

Again it was sometimes argued that the Tolai like to take their wet beans to Rabaul whenever they want to make a purchase in order to have ready cash available on the spot. Saturday is the day on which most people make their way to Rabaul to visit the market (see Ch. 7). Yet none of the project fermentaries accepts wet beans at the weekend. In order to overcome this disadvantage, the project started a buying station at Rabaul market in 1966. It operated for three months, but was then discontinued because it was found uneconomic.

Another reason often advanced to explain the cocoa sales pattern is that the growers prefer a larger immediate cash payment—in 1960 the project offered a down payment of 6d. while Chinese traders paid once and for all 7d. per pound of wet beans—rather than waiting to receive their final payments twice yearly from the project. In 1960 the final payment by the project amounted to almost 2d. per wet bean pound. This meant that every pound of cocoa sold to Chinese traders involved the grower in 1d. loss, quite apart from possible short weighing. In the short run the grower gained, while in the long run he obviously lost by selling to independent traders. The larger immediate cash payment might have accounted for growers preferring to sell to traders if there had been a shortage of ready cash. However, Tolai on the whole were, and still are, extremely thrifty and most of them have accumulated cash savings—some even have considerable bank accounts—therefore more ready cash in hand cannot be taken to have supplied sufficient inducement to many to forego larger returns in the long run.

What then may be the deciding factor for so much cocoa being sold outside the project? This question has puzzled many of the people concerned. Some regard cocoa sales to Chinese traders as a sign of plain irrationality; others attribute it to sheer contrariness. The most outspoken critics of 'irresponsible' attitudes are some leading Tolai themselves. They castigate their fellow tribesmen most severely. I attended one meeting in 1960, held at Rapitok fermentary, where one of the most respected elders in the area encouraged his audience of cocoa growers to beat up anyone they found taking wet beans to traders rather than to the project. If they were taken to court he empowered them to tell the administrative officer concerned that he, their elder, had ordered them to take steps against their irresponsible and foolish tribesmen and that he was prepared to accept full responsibility for their actions. This speech might be taken to indicate that there was political opposition between supporters of the project and those who sell outside it: that the drift away from the fermentaries represented a break-away political movement. However, while the project supporters openly declared their loyalty to council fermentaries, those who sold their cocoa to traders almost always did so secretly: they collected their wet beans early in the morning and then took them to traders under shelter of darkness. There has, as yet, not been any overt movement of Tolai declaring openly that they wished to sell their cocoa outside the project.

Rapitok Cocoa Production and Sales

In order to show the pattern of overall cocoa production and sales, I shall focus attention once more on Rapitok. In 1960, 60 per cent of the 144 households cultivated some cocoa trees, but only 54 per cent had bearing trees. There was a wide range in the number planted by individual households: it varied from 112 to 2,990; 21 per cent of the cocoa-growing households had less than 400 trees, while 23 per cent had more than 1,000 (see Table 20). Altogether there were 46,000 bearing trees and 20,000 non-bearing trees in 1960, as counted by my Rapitok assistants under my supervision,* although according to records compiled by the Department of Agriculture in Rabaul, Rapitok had altogether no more than 11,855 cocoa trees at that time.† However, I saw registration certi-

* Totals have been rounded up to the nearest thousand; for precise numbers see Table 11.

† Communication received from the Department of Agriculture, Rabaul, dated 17/10/66.

ficates for about 35,000. In spite of the fact that the 1952 Cocoa Ordinance makes it compulsory for growers to register their trees with the Department of Agriculture, as many as 24 per cent of the 46,000 mature cocoa trees in Rapitok were grown without legal registration.

Table 20

Distribution of cocoa trees among Rapitok households, 1960

Nos. of cocoa trees	Households	
	No.	%
1– 199	6	7
200– 399	12	14
400– 599	19	22
600– 799	21	24
800– 999	9	10
1,000–1,199	8	9
1,200 and over	12	14
Total	87	100

In order to gauge cultivators' income from cocoa I first copied the records of Rapitok fermentary relating to residents; and second, I closely observed all wet beans taken out of Rapitok in the four months' period between March and June 1960 and checked on quantity sold and amounts received. On many occasions I went to Rabaul with growers who were taking their wet beans to Chinese traders, but in accordance with their request I kept discreetly in the background so that neither the Chinese trader nor other Tolai would become aware of my presence. In these four months cultivators sold approximately 28,500 lb. wet beans to independent traders for which they received about £850. March to June are peak months in the production of cocoa, and I estimate that cocoa sales during this period constitute 40 per cent of annual sales to traders. This estimate is based on the relationship between the annual quantity of wet beans growers brought to the fermentary and that which they delivered there during the four peak months. Accordingly, I estimate that 71,000 lb. wet beans were sold to independent traders during the period October 1959 to September 1960 and that at the rate of 7d. per pound of wet beans (which the traders were paying) they received about £2,100. During the same period the Rapitok fermentary records show that cultivators sold 158,600 lb. wet beans to the project for which they received a total of £5,375. During the first half of the period the project paid 8d. per pound wet beans while during the second half 8·25d.*

Eight of the seventy-eight Rapitok households with bearing cocoa trees in 1960—that is 10 per cent—had not bothered to enrol with the project; they were taking all their wet beans to Chinese traders. The seventy households which had enrolled with the local fermentary accounted for eighty-seven individual names and numbers on the fermentary register; thirteen households had two separate registrations and two households had as many as three. Where a household had more than one name registered with the fermentary the additional names were those of young sons or sometimes daughters entered by the father so as to provide them with an independent source of income. This shows the Tolai fathers' attempts to secure their children's future in opposition to the traditional system of matrilineal inheritance.

Matrilineal Inheritance and Cocoa Sales

A considerable number of Rapitok men, who have had their own matrilineage lands planted with cocoa by their sons, wish to conceal this fact from their fellow parishioners. The dilemma and difficulties of a father emerge clearly from the following case history of one householder, with whom I had many long talks during which he unburdened his troubled mind, and whose activities I closely observed. In order to preserve his anonymity I shall call him To Tama and his son To Bul.

To Tama is a man who in 1960 was in his early fifties. He

* A cross-check on Rapitok's overall cocoa production in 1959/60 confirms that about 30 per cent of the cocoa produced was sold outside the project. Since the annual average yield of wet beans per cocoa tree is about 5 lb., approximately 32,000 cocoa trees could produce the 158,600 lb. wet beans which growers supplied to their local fermentary. The produce of the remaining 14,000 bearing trees — 30 per cent — was sold to independent traders.

was married to a woman from Napapar, a neighbouring parish, and had one son, who was then 25 years old, as well as two younger daughters. He had two younger sisters; one of them was married in Napapar and had two sons and one daughter; the other was married in Tinganagalip and had two daughters. To Tama's descent-group controlled a considerable area of land in Rapitok, whereas his wife's kin-group was not represented at all in the parish. His son, To Bul, had, therefore, no recognised claim to any land in Rapitok. To Tama planted 510 cocoa trees on his matrilineage lands, which he registered in 1955 with the Department of Agriculture, according to the law. However, in the same year he encouraged his son To Bul to help him plant more cocoa trees on another (not adjacent) area of land also vested in his own kin-group. Father and son jointly planted another 417 trees, which they did not register in order to avoid having to commit themselves about their ownership of the trees. To Tama did not want members of his own descent-group to become aware that he intended these trees for his son, nor did he want a document among his treasures indicating his name as owner of all the 927 cocoa trees (see p. 130). When the trees began to bear To Tama registered with the local fermentary and since then he has taken about half the produce of the trees to the fermentary. The rest he or his son regularly take to Chinese traders in Rabaul and the proceeds are kept by To Bul. In 1960 To Tama was about to arrange To Bul's marriage to a Rapitok girl, the daughter of another Napapar woman married to a Rapitok man. He hoped To Bul would settle down in Rapitok and eventually inherit all his father's cocoa and coconut gardens. In the meantime, however, he made certain that To Bul was at least able to accumulate the proceeds from half his cocoa trees by secretly selling these wet beans to Chinese traders. To Tama, otherwise a law-abiding Tolai, was caught in the dilemma created by the contradictory pulls emanating from his relationship with his kin-group on the one hand and with his son on the other.

In a small society such as Rapitok, everyone inevitably knows almost all of everyone else's business. Although To Tama has avoided any written record of his son's cocoa enterprise, most Rapitoks were aware of it. There was always a potential source of friction between To Tama and members of his own descent-group on the one hand, and between them and his son backed by the latter's kin-group on the other. This tension flared up into open conflict from time to time over different issues quite apart from landholding and cocoa trees. It will definitely become acute and overt on To Tama's death, when his inheritance will have to be settled and competing interests will state their claims openly. A great deal will then depend on the comparative status in the area of the leading elders involved (see p. 109).

Boundaries between pieces of land belonging to different kin-groups had not been clearly defined or marked in 1960; leading elders provided the key to the landholding pattern. The absence of registered titles to land still allowed considerable flexibility in recognising claims to land by different individuals. Furthermore, the custom according to which next of kin of a deceased could stake a claim to some of his property by distributing tambu at his mortuary rite provided another means for sons to inherit their fathers' perennial tree crops. In order to provide the best possible chance for his son to keep charge of the cocoa trees that have been planted on To Tama's matrilineal lands, the father tried to keep no record of these trees or the proceeds from them. He tried as best he could to mystify future elders in Rapitok who will be called upon to arbitrate the competing claims to his property which he expects to arise on his death. To Tama realised that all he could possibly do was delay the hour of decision over his son's claim. However, in the meantime at least, the income from To Bul's clandestine cocoa sales to traders was accumulating in the young man's own savings account without there being in existence any record of the origin of this money. Therefore, on To Tama's death his matrilineal kin would not be able to claim this money as theirs.

To Tama is one of a number of Rapitok men—and I suspect also one of a great many Tolai all over the Gazelle Peninsula—who is on the whole respected and upright, but who is forced by circumstances beyond his control to act against the generally accepted code of his society. It obviously worried him that he was obliged to trick members of his own descent-group by allowing his son to cultivate part of their lands and letting him cash and keep the proceeds. Moreover, he felt ashamed of having to take his cocoa secretly to Chinese traders under cover of darkness. He would have liked to be able to give the project his wholehearted support. He appreciated that not only did it pay more in the long run than independent traders but it also represented an enterprise which he regarded as worthy of his support. Yet he could see no way out of his dilemma. To Tama appeared to be one of many caught in similar difficult circumstances.

In 1960 of the seventy-eight Rapitok households with mature cocoa trees only 64 per cent sold all their wet beans to the project; 26 per cent sold partly to the project and partly to Chinese traders, in the way To Tama did; 10 per cent did not even bother to register as suppliers to the local fermentary and took all their cocoa to traders. Altogether twenty-eight Rapitok households sold part or all of their wet beans to Chinese traders. According to data which I collected, 86 per cent of them did so to provide for their sons, just as To Tama was doing, while the remaining 14 per cent sold to Chinese mainly in order to get hold of what was then illicit liquor. Similarly, the considerable proportion of cocoa trees not registered with the Department of Agriculture can probably be accounted for by fathers wanting to have their own matrilineage land cultivated by their sons. Tolai wrongly believed that the 'licence' for cocoa trees represented a legal title to ownership. That this was so is evidenced by the following remarks which were written by a Tolai and published in the *Project News Sheet,* No. 11 (1960). This article was written for the cocoa growers who did not understand what 'cocoa registration' meant and for those who intended to grow cocoa in future. It was based on complaints brought before the district agricultural officer at Taliligap by a group of people.

> In the Gazelle Peninsula, about twice as many of the cocoa gardens belonging to natives are owned by groups of people known as clan or *vunatarai.* For these people, the garden is registered under one name, that is usually the leader of the clan. This kind of ownership is very hard to follow for the European because there are many people involved in the

ownership. Very often disputes occur amongst these people.

Recently, a group of people came and complained to the District Agricultural Officer, that one of their relatives, who had never done any work to the garden since its clearing, had tried to inherit the whole property for himself. By right, he was the next leader, but because he had never done any work, his relatives disliked him for his laziness and wanted to ostracize him.

However, they brought with them the 'licence' (Certificate of Registration) to show the District Agricultural Officer and get the assurance that while they have this piece in their possesssion they think they have the rights and power to ostracize anyone of their clan . . .

The growers must remember that the Certificate of Registration or licence, as it is known to growers, gives no title over the ownership of gardens. Likewise, in a clan, the leader, who has his name registered for the garden, and having possession of this paper, has not the power to deal with any lazy individuals in his clan and try to discard them from clan ownership by virtue of anything contained in it.

Any dispute or dislikes among the people over the ownership is entirely their own affair . . .

It is a very common thing in the *vunatarai* in the Tolai area to have disputes, dislikes and jealousy over land and garden ownership.

We must remember that farming is a business enterprise and we should think first before planning to make a garden. All who are concerned with making a big garden should have one mind so as to avoid trouble in future.

Thus we see that the belief that a cocoa 'licence' provided a title to land was not limited to Rapitok but appeared to be held throughout the whole society. Many fathers did not want to rigidify the inheritance of land by committing ownership of cocoa gardens to paper. Like To Tama they wanted to keep the system of claims to land flexible. In fact all they were doing was delaying the decision over competing claims. This then may account for the large and apparently growing discrepancy between the number of registered cocoa trees and actual plantings. According to Williamson in 1954/5 only 41 per cent of all Tolai cocoa trees had been registered with the Department of Agriculture (1958: 595). A rough estimate of the number of mature cocoa trees in 1965 based on total dry cocoa production divided by 2·2 lb., being the average productivity per mature cocoa tree, indicates a considerable discrepancy between the total number of registered cocoa trees — 3,623,058 — and the then mature cocoa trees in the area — 4,241,800. The total number of registered cocoa trees represented only 85 per cent of the already mature trees in 1965 (see Table 19). The difference between the last two columns in Table 23 clearly indicates that the proportion of cocoa trees registered under the cocoa ordinance has actually been declining over the years. The growing population pressure on land appears to have made more and more Tolai reluctant to commit themselves, as they thought, to the title to land.

Moreover, the increasing proportion of land cultivated by men squatting on the lands of their fathers' matrilineage can also account for the increasing drift away from the project. The Tolai concerned want to avoid any record of their income from the sale of wet beans. An event which occurred in Rabaul in the early 1960s and which was related to me by a reliable informant bears out the people's extreme distrust of cocoa sales records. The Tolai Cocoa Project had requested police action against the increasing proportion of cocoa sold to Chinese traders. Although the police had no legal powers to stop such sales, it was arranged for native policemen, who were illiterate, to stand outside the chief Chinese cocoa buying points. Their duties were to pretend to keep records of truck numbers as well as the amount of cocoa sold to Chinese traders. The Tolai were fully aware that the police had no legal powers to stop them selling their cocoa to expatriate traders. Nevertheless, as a result of this simple police action, the majority of Tolai concerned took most of their cocoa to the project fermentaries. The resulting loss of Chinese trade in cocoa was so severe that Chinese businessmen in Rabaul threatened legal action unless the policemen were withdrawn. Accordingly, the policemen were recalled and the drift away from the project once more assumed considerable proportion. This incident shows that it was the anonymity of sales which attracted Tolai to sell to independent traders. As soon as they thought that records were kept of their sales to Chinese buyers they seemed to prefer to sell to the project. This was certainly true of a number of Rapitok growers and probably applied to many other Tolai as well.

Though I have no directly comparable data from other parishes as regards the cocoa sales pattern, it seems reasonable to assume that the Rapitok sales behaviour is representative of the whole community. The somewhat smaller percentage of cocoa sold to Chinese in 1959/60 from Rapitok — 31 per cent — than the 40 per cent sold outside the project by Tolai cocoa producers as a whole can readily be explained by the fact that Rapitok, in contrast to many other Tolai settlements, had as yet no serious land shortage. Therefore, the pressure to sell to traders was not as strong there as in other settlements.

The Rapitok data clearly show that the complex pattern of landholding and inheritance constitutes the crux of the drift away from the project. There were, no doubt, a number of other contributory factors. Yet none of these individual factors could possibly account for the increasing proportion of cocoa sales to independent traders. The increasing drift away from the project was in fact largely a result of the difficulties arising from the introduction of perennial cash crops into a society with a traditional social system according to which inheritance followed the matrilineal line of descent, whereas residence was patri-virilocal. The rapid growth of population, accompanied by extensive cash cropping, accounted for the increasing demand and competition for land. Sons could no longer be accommodated in their fathers' parish according to the customary system of landholding, unless they had claims to land there on the basis of their own descent-group.

On the basis of the foregoing argument it is easy to predict that within the next decade or so, when a large proportion of the present Tolai elders are likely to die, there will be a flood of land disputes sweeping across parishes, unless titles to land have been sorted out by then.

The increasing land shortage is likely to make things more and more difficult for the Tolai in general and the project in particular. A radical change in the whole basis of land ownership would be required to uproot the traditional control over land. Such radical change would, no doubt, be active in revolutionising the whole social structure. However, unless this is done or the project is re-organised so as to abolish growers' sales records, the Tolai Cocoa Project will have to prepare itself for a continuing decline in the proportion of cocoa it will handle.

7

Rabaul Market

In the previous chapter I discussed how, where, and why Rapitok cultivators sold their wet cocoa beans. It emerged that the integration of the Tolai into the wider cash economy was affected by their customary social and economic system and that in turn this integration may affect the form of traditional organisation. To demonstrate the mutual interaction between the new economic opportunities and Tolai traditional organisation I now want to discuss their activities as market vendors. We have seen that markets are by no means new institutions: there were chains of markets even in pre-contact days, when tambu was used as a measure of value and a medium of exchange. However, in the past most markets were intra-Tolai, whereas nowadays the increasing number of expatriates as well as of natives from other parts of New Guinea and Papua provide a growing market for Tolai food produce. Moreover, by contrast with pre-contact times when the major incentive to market selling was the accumulation of tambu, the bulk of market trade is now conducted with cash and many a vendor produces for and sells at the market simply because he wants the cash either for saving or for purchasing a certain article in the town shops.

The following discussion is based on a study of sellers I conducted at Rabaul market in June 1961.* Each Saturday morning almost all Tolai-owned trucks, jeeps and utilities, as well as many non-native-owned vehicles hired by Tolai, con-

* The survey was conducted in conjunction with Dr R. Salisbury, who concerned himself with studying the demand side of the market, while I concentrated on supply.

verged on Rabaul — many of them made several trips — to bring women with their produce to the market. It would certainly be true to say that on Saturdays in the Gazelle Peninsula all roads lead to Rabaul. The first sellers arrived about 5 a.m. and from then onwards there was a constant stream of sellers arriving at the market until about 9 a.m. The market, referred to by natives and non-natives alike by the vernacular term *bung,* was held on an open piece of land, an area of about one and a third acres. The land was vested in the Rabaul Native Local Government Council; it nestled against the hills in the background and bordered the main Chinese shopping streets. There were two sheds, the larger of which, measuring about 240 square yards, was used for the display of European and Chinese types of produce, such as lettuce, tomatoes, cabbages and the like; the smaller shed of about 100 square yards was rarely used at all, except for native buyers who wanted to shelter either from the burning sun or from tropical downpours of rain. Most sellers squatted on the ground and placed their produce in bundles on leaves in front of them, or they displayed their wares on rough bamboo tables and themselves settled down on the ground in the shade of the tables. Most of the vendors were women, some of them selling produce on behalf of their menfolk. Only about 2 per cent of the sellers on a Saturday and no more than 1 per cent on weekdays were men.

There were no rules laid down as to who may settle down where. Yet over the years a convention had developed by which each parish usually occupied a certain position in the market place (see Map V). Moreover, there was also a certain specialisation of produce according to parishes — for example, Matupi women sold mainly fish, wild fowl eggs, and lime, while Rapitok women sold taro, sweet potatoes, and yams — there was thus, to some extent, an order of seating according to produce. However, this specialisation based on the correlation between the different parishes and their different produce was by no means complete. Some vendors distributed their wares over a number of different places in the market and had them watched by their female friends or relatives. For instance, Matupi women frequently brought beans, lime, and cooked fish to the market; they placed the beans in the European-

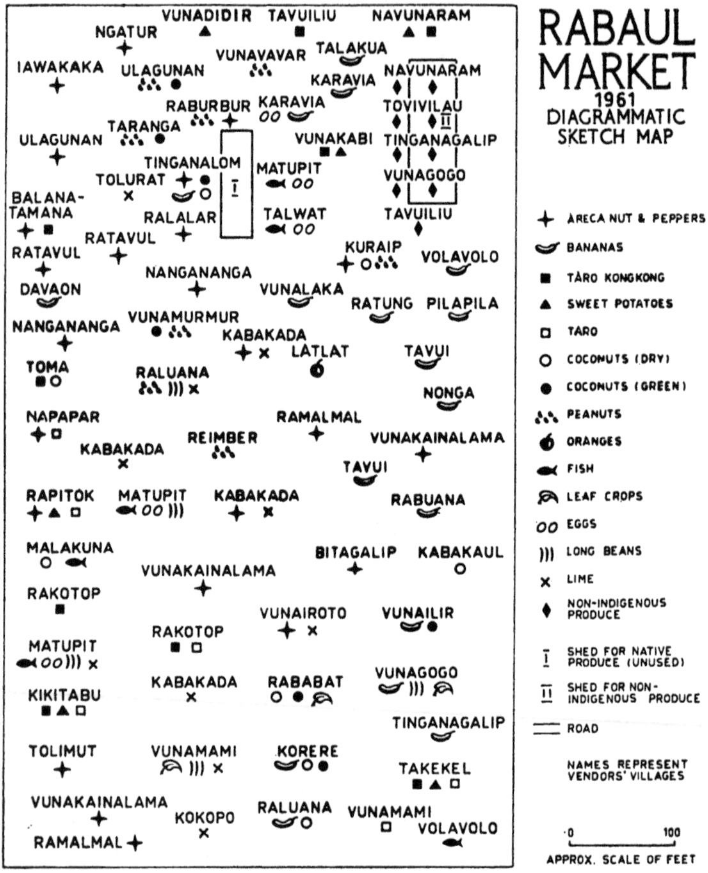

V *Diagrammatic sketch map of Rabaul market, 1961*

and Chinese-type produce shed under the supervision of relatives from Tinganagalip; the lime was watched by Raluana friends, while they squatted down and offered their cooked fish for sale. At intervals they went round to visit the various places where they had deposited their produce and collected the cash or tambu received for the sale of their goods. There was a constant movement of sellers between different places in the market. Many women vendors left their produce in the care of one or two of their friends or relatives while they went off to the town to shop. The Tolai obviously regarded the *bung* not only as a place where goods may be bought and sold, but even more as a social meeting place. Men and women from the many different settlements exchanged news and gossip; they arranged bride purchases and fixed or announced the dates of feasts and mortuary rites. Many women brought just enough produce to the market to pay for their transport to Rabaul. For them the visit to the market was not so much an economic enterprise as a social outing.

A great number of different types of food was sold at Rabaul market. I counted at least fifty, not including the varieties within each type (for example, there were more than ten different kinds of bananas sold). My survey showed that in 1961 on a Saturday there were slightly more than 2,000 sellers gathered at Rabaul and the turnover was approximately £2,750. The great number of individual vendors and the great variety of produce sold made it practically impossible for one or two research workers to conduct the study on their own, but I was fortunate enough to get several Tolai agricultural field assistants as well as some Tolai teachers to help me.* My purpose in studying Rabaul market was twofold: firstly, to examine the price-forming mechanism, to find out how sellers arrived at a price, which by previous observation I had found to be almost uniform for the same commodity all over the market on any one day; secondly, to find out the part the market played in the overall economy.

Survey Techniques

I am not aware of any generally accepted technique of studying markets, particularly native markets in underdeveloped areas, so I describe here the techniques I employed in the Rabaul market survey. Since most vendors arrived by some means of motor transport, I had one man posted at the road corner, which most vehicles entering the market had to pass. This man noted the number and type of each vehicle entering the market:

* I am indebted to Mr J. Berry and Mr B. Johnston, both of the Department of Agriculture, Rabaul, for their help in providing me with a considerable number of field assistants. My thanks are also due to those assistants and to the ten Tolai teachers, who volunteered to help on Saturdays. Moreover, I am grateful to the many vendors who volunteered detailed information.

truck, jeep, utility, etc. Four assistants, each posted at different sides of the market square, noted the type of vehicle arriving, the number of female vendors disembarking, and the parish from which they came. The rest of my assistants, about twenty in all, were placed randomly all over the market area. Each was equipped with a number of schedules and recorded the following details of sellers and their sales throughout their stay at the market:

1. name, home parish, type of transport, and fare paid;
2. time of arrival and number as well as price of each item brought for sale;
3. particulars of each sale made, indicating time, number and price as well as the ethnic group of the buyer, i.e., whether European, Chinese, Papuan, New Guinean or Tolai;
4. The quantity of each item unsold when the vendor left the market.

Each assistant recorded the details of three or four sellers in this way.

In order to establish the relationship between the random sample and the total universe from which the sample was drawn, I counted the total number of sellers present at the market at about 9 a.m. on each day of my survey. The count of the women who had come to the market by motor transport provided me with a rough idea of the number of vendors. However, not all women who arrived by vehicle were actual sellers, nor did all sellers arrive by motor transport. On the Saturdays surveyed, about 5 per cent of the women vendors walked to the market. The first people arrived at the market at about 5 a.m.; the whole market came to life only about 8 a.m. A count of sellers at 9 a.m. seemed the only reliable way of ascertaining the total number on any one market day, because very few left before that time, nor did many arrive later. However, in order to make certain that my calculations included all market vendors, I made a 10 per cent allowance on the total number I counted present at the market at 9 a.m. on each survey day. This 10 per cent margin sets an upper limit to include all temporary absentees as well as errors in enumeration.

On weekdays there was much less activity at the *bung* than on Saturdays, though weekday trading was steadily increasing. In 1960, the year before my survey, hardly any trade had been conducted during the week, while in June 1961 the average turnover on each weekday was about £110. The task of surveying the market during the week, however, was relatively easy. The survey was started on 1 June and conducted for one whole week. In order to check the reliability of the first Saturday's findings, I conducted another survey on the third Saturday in June. This showed very similar results and thus bears out, at least to some degree, the replicability of the data obtained.

However, before any conclusions can be drawn from the findings of this survey as to the annual market turnover, a few reservations must be made. Firstly, there are seasonal variations in agricultural output, particularly in European- and Chinese-type produce. Normally, the flush begins in June and reaches its peak in August, whereas January and February are months of scarcity when least produce reaches the market and prices are highest. Secondly, within the seasonal variations there were random differences from week to week. For instance, during the first week of my survey there was not a single fish offered for sale, whereas on the second Saturday the market was well supplied with fish. Matupi fishermen had been unsuccessful during the first week in June 1961, whereas they managed to make an excellent catch two weeks later. These are important reservations when we come to examine the part the market played in the overall economy.

The Price-forming Mechanism

Most items were sold in 1/- bundles; nothing was sold by weight. The convention of selling in terms of monetary units rather than by weight made trading a lot easier but it also created certain difficulties. It was much easier to calculate prices in set units of 1/- rather than to have to add up pence and shillings; with items such as beans, which are small and where the quantity could be easily varied to change the price, no difficulty arose. Only when it came to items such as paw-paws or pineapples, which varied considerably in size, weight and quality, problems arose over the price. For instance, I weighed two papaws: one weighed 15 lb., the other only 5 lb., yet each was offered for sale at the same price of 1/-. However, very big pineapples were sometimes sold for 2/- each.

Price differences were apparent only in the variation of the quantities of produce offered in 1/- lots. Many sellers prepared their bundles before they reached the market, either before they left their home parish or on the way to the market. There was a clear distinction between the price mechanism as it operated with European-and Chinese-type produce, on the one hand and native produce on the other.

(a) *Non-indigenous foods*

At the beginning of each market day prices varied between different vendors, though only slightly. This was so because vendors gauged the size of the 1/- lots they prepared for sale by the supply offered from their own parish. For instance, if several vendors took lettuce to the market from Tinganagalip, the women from that parish arranged 1/- bundles each containing three lettuces. If, on reaching the market, they found that other parishes had also a flush of lettuce on that day while demand was not very brisk, each vendor increased the size of her 1/- bundles to contain four or sometimes even five lettuces. They thereby reduced the price per lettuce from 4d. to 3d. or even less. On any one market day the supply price of produce was determined by those vendors who came from the parish which supplied most of the particular item. The actual selling price then depended on the extent of the demand. However, this applied only if buyers were not willing to purchase at the prices asked by vendors. Slack demand tended to decrease the sale price: by contrast, brisk demand had no immediate upward effect on prices. For instance, if Tinganagalip vendors arrived at the market and found that they were among very few sellers of lettuce, while demand for lettuce was extensive, they never reduced the size of their 1/- bundles to contain only two lettuces.

The existence of immediate downward flexibility of market prices without the concomitant immediate price increases as a result of demand influences may at first appear inconsistent.

However, it is readily understood if we bear in mind that gauging the extent of demand is a very tricky operation which requires shrewd commercial knowledge. There are probably very few market gardeners indeed in the whole world who have sufficient business experience to raise their prices if the state of demand and supply allows it. It is much more obvious to vendors when their prices are too high than when they are too low. If a Rabaul market seller was left with a large part of her produce unsold for any length of time, she began to worry and look around; then, if she noticed other vendors increasing the size of their 1/- bundles, she followed suit, thereby reducing the price. On the other hand, if she found a rush on her produce, as was frequently the case with tomatoes, she had little time either to look around to check upon the overall supply of tomatoes available for sale at the market, nor had she time to reduce the size of her already prepared 1/- bundles.

A few enterprising coastal Tolai women acted as middlemen in trade: they bought tomatoes, onions, lettuce, beans and other non-native types of produce at the market and hawked them round European and Chinese stores and private homes. European and Chinese shop employees and some housewives who did not manage to get to the market were pleased to have this opportunity of buying fresh vegetables and did not mind paying a little more for the service rendered them by these street hawkers. By reducing the size of the 1/- bundles these intermediary traders made about one-third profit. In the course of my survey I observed on a number of occasions coastal women each buying ten small baskets of tomatoes at the market for 1/- each, then re-arranging them into fifteen lots and hawking these round the town. After some time they returned to the market with their takings of 15/-.

There were certain indications that the sellers based the size of their 1/- bundles on the experience they gained of supply and demand as it had operated on their previous visit to the *bung*. Not a single vendor regarded market selling as a full-time occupation and came regularly every day: most of them appeared only on Saturdays, a few also came once or twice during the week. I observed three vendors who came to sell their tomatoes on Monday and again on Wednesday. On their first visit to the market that week they had each prepared five small baskets containing two large and four small tomatoes, which they managed to sell immediately on arrival at the market. Very few tomatoes were offered for sale on that Monday and a number of European and Chinese buyers were looking for them. Two days later, the very same vendors arrived again at the market; this time they each brought eight baskets in each of which were only one large and three small tomatoes. But they were unlucky, for on that day there were plenty of tomatoes available and demand was slack. In the course of the day they had to increase the size of their 1/- lots so that they sold six instead of eight bundles apiece. They left the market each with 6/- takings instead of the expected 8/-.

Buyers looking for bargains were well advised to come to the market in the afternoon, when sellers wanted to pack up and were prepared to reduce their prices by increasing the size of their lots. A major drawback of late afternoon buying was, however, that by then the best quality produce had been sold. Yet there was a minimum price below which very few sellers were prepared to sell: they preferred to take their unsold produce home rather than sell it at what they regarded as unreasonably low prices. I watched some Chinese, the shrewdest buyers of all, trying late on a Saturday afternoon to buy for 2/- three 1/- bundles of lettuce, each containing four lettuces. They were refused by one vendor after another. The sellers preferred to throw the lettuces away — very few Tolai themselves eat lettuce — rather than sell them at what they regarded as too low a price.

No vendor ever attempted to undercut her neighbour's prices. It was this which made for the uniformity in prices all over the market on any one day. In this respect Rabaul market differed distinctly from any Asian market, or even from the market at Camden Town, London, where many barrow boys on a Saturday try to sell their wares to bargain hunters. At Rabaul market the prospective buyer could walk around examining the goods offered by as many sellers as he wished without being invited to buy at any of their stalls, whereas in Asia or at Camden Town anyone walking through the market is solicited by each and every seller, who tries to impress on the buyer the superior quality and lower prices of his own goods as compared with any other goods on the market. The Tolai seller did not offer her goods for sale beyond displaying them to prospective buyers, nor was she prepared to bargain. On one occasion, I watched the Indian cook of a ship docked in Rabaul harbour trying to bargain when buying fruit and vegetables for his ship, but he was completely unsuccessful. His attempts to bargain by offering to buy large quantities of produce failed to arouse any interest at all. He had to pay the price demanded or leave the produce behind. Consequently he bought a lot less than he had intended to buy.

On walking through the market one got the impression of facing a body of monopolistic sellers rather than a large number of small individual vendors in competition with each other. The sellers looked as if they were not at all keen to sell their produce. Many a vendor packed up her unsold non-indigenous types of produce at about 10.30 a.m. and started hawking it round the town shops and houses. Here, too, there were usually a few women sellers going round together, each with their individual produce, without ever attempting to compete with each other.

This lack of competitive spirit and absence of 'sales drive' may be explained by a number of different but interdependent factors. Most important was the fact that all market vendors were selling their own produce; there were no professional traders at all. Therefore none of the vendors was dependent for her livelihood on her income from trading. Moreover, as we have seen, Tolai, in particular those coming from the interior (who supplied most fruit and vegetables to the market), were still living by subsistence production and their cash requirements were limited. There was thus not the urgency or incentive for sellers to maximise their gains by underbidding their neighbours. Market trade was regarded as a welcome addition to cash or tambu wealth rather than as a necessary means to earning a living. Furthermore, social considerations counterbalanced economic incentives. The widespread network of social relations reduced the desire for sellers to compete with each other. Since vendors coming from the same parish usually settled down next to each other in the market place, and offered mostly identical produce, sellers sitting in one vicinity were usually relatives, as well as friends and neighbours. Besides, the Tolai matrilineal kinship system, coupled with patri-virilocal residence, results in a widespread inter-parish network of kinship and friendship relations between women from quite different areas. For instance, I saw one woman placing her small baskets of tomatoes in the care of another seller. The first one was from Volavolo on the north-west coast of the Gazelle Peninsula and the second was from Tinganagalip, about 10 miles south-west of Rabaul and about 16 miles from Volavolo. When I inquired how the two women had got to know each other, they explained that they were affines; the first one was born and had grown up in Raluana, a coastal parish about 5 miles south of Rabaul; she had married into Tinganagalip, while the second was from Tinganagalip and had married into Volavolo. It never occurred to the Tinganagalip vendor, who looked after her own tomatoes as well as those belonging to the Volavolo woman, to induce buyers to purchase her own produce in preference to that brought by her affine, nor did she try to increase the size of her own small baskets of tomatoes to attract buyers to purchase her own rather than those belonging to the other vendor. Thus the network of kinship and personal relations further neutralises competition.

According to custom it was regarded as bad form to display greed in getting rewards or payment. Parkinson wrote that

> . . . it is interesting to watch large payments of tambu being made or tambu distributions at feasts and to note the complete indifference displayed by those who pay or distribute the large sums of the highly treasured tambu, as well as by those who receive it, who do not look at it but leave it untouched lying next to themselves as if they had some inner repulsion to picking it up. All this, however, is only pretence, because there is nothing in the world which means more to the native than tambu (1906: 88).

This mode of behaviour still persisted in 1961. Frequently, it was not even the vendor herself who accepted payment for produce sold, but her neighbour, who subsequently handed the money over to her. Men regarded it as bad form if their womenfolk showed any eagerness at the market to sell their produce.

There were probably other contributory factors which helped to account for the absence of competition at Rabaul market. However, I regard the three discussed above as the most important and decisive in this context. The monopolistic behaviour of a large number of small individual vendors was largely due to a combination of economic and social factors. Economically the Tolai were too wealthy and socially too well integrated to allow for outright competition between sellers. The attraction of going to Rabaul and meeting friends and relatives from other parishes discouraged the development of professional traders in the area. From an economic point of view it would have been much more efficient either for women from one parish to combine their produce and delegate only one or two to take it to the market, or for a few trucks to go round the area buying up the produce at point of origin and retailing on the market. Such arrangement would have resulted in much better organised and more profitable trade. Yet no such attempts were made by anyone, simply because women producers were not interested in subordinating the social advantages of their market visits to economic gains.

Unfortunately, there were no records available of price movements at Rabaul market over the years. Nevertheless, there were some indications that prices had been rising steadily, at least since the last war. An article in the *Pacific Islands Monthly* of 1950 brought out two interesting facts in this respect (Rhodes, 1950: 69). The writer complained that the same quantity of tomatoes or beans which could be bought immediately after the war with a stick of tobacco, the price of which was 6d., cost 1/- in 1950. This showed two things: firstly, it clearly indicated a rise in prices, though no quantities were specified to enable comparison between 1950 and 1961 prices. The article hinted that the reason for the rising prices was that the Tolai were getting wise to being exploited by the Chinese in their trade stores and therefore, wanting to get their own back, were raising their prices in the market, where most buyers were Chinese. Rhodes, however, ignored the fact of a general rising price level during that period, coupled with a growing pattern of Tolai wants and an increasing European and Chinese population. Secondly, the article clearly brought out the change-over from a semi-barter economy, where non-Tolai buyers paid with tobacco, to a largely cash economy, where cash was the major medium of exchange.

As we have seen in pre-contact days, exchange among the Tolai had been facilitated by tambu. After first European contact, when the Tolai began to appreciate the white man's goods, they became eager to accept payment for their produce in tobacco, tools, or weapons. Pullen-Burry, who visited the Gazelle Peninsula in 1906, described a native market at a plantation near Kokopo where natives were paid

> for edible commodities with sticks of coarse tobacco, which is dearly loved by them. I saw three eggs taken from an old woman who produced them from some hidden receptacle in her scanty, but filthy clothing, and she was given two sticks in return, and seemed well satisfied (1909: 95).

Thus it would seem that from the earliest days of European contact until after the last war, the major means of payment was in fact tobacco. This contrasts sharply with the fact that during the whole time of my market survey there was not a single transaction between Tolai vendors and non-Tolai buyers conducted in any other medium save cash. The very recent conversion of the link between the Tolai and the wider economy from semi-barter to wholly cash demonstrates the rapid and extremely recent economic progress of the Tolai.

It would have been interesting to discover the long-term reaction of supply to price changes, that is to say, whether or not growers varied the quantity they cultivated in line with prices prevailing at the time of planting. However, there are as yet no data available on this problem, nor was it possible for me to collect this information in the short time at my disposal.

(b) *Indigenous foods*

We have already noted that the Tolai had been trading their produce long before European contact. This trade was brought about by the different yet complementary ecology of coastal and inland Tolai and was facilitated by tambu. Danks, the first European resident missionary in the Tolai area, reported in 1887

> Market is held on the coast every third day in a large number of places. Those who live very far back inland have their inland markets where they sell to those nearer the beach who in turn sell what they buy to the coastal people. These markets are so arranged that two are seldom held near each other on the same day. A man taking his produce to one market today, may take more to another tomorrow if he is so disposed, and if it is safe for him to do so. The coast people meet the inland people at these markets with their fish and articles of European manufacture and either sell them for tambu or barter for food and other things only obtainable in the country (1887: 315).

In addition, Tolai were accustomed to employing a generally accepted medium of exchange rather than using straight barter. Tambu, as we have seen, was the most desired object. No man was held in greater contempt than a spendthrift. Though after some years of European contact the people became adjusted to the idea of accepting at first trade goods and eventually cash in payment for their produce and labour sold to Europeans, tambu remained for a long time the major medium of all intra-Tolai trade. In 1961 25 per cent of all intra-Tolai transactions on a Saturday at Rabaul market was still conducted in tambu rather than cash. By convention the Tolai usually buy certain native-type produce mainly with tambu: for instance almost all cooked food such as fish and tapioca, *imbika* (*Abelmoschu manihot*, native spinach), peanuts, lime and taro were mostly bought with tambu.

The economic system in fact consisted of three sectors: the subsistence, the tambu, and the cash sector. Tambu formed the connecting link between them. Food could be bought with tambu and sold for cash and vice versa. Tambu was thus a highly liquid asset. Yet it was extremely difficult to assess its money equivalent. First of all, Tolai still clung to the purely arbitrary rate of one fathom equalling 2/-, which was a carry-over from German times when one fathom was equated with 2 marks. However, while the purchasing power of cash has fallen much more than that of tambu during the last sixty years and the cash price of tambu at Nakanai, its source, has more than doubled in the same period, Tolai still quoted this customary exchange rate. This clearly indicates that in practice they were not particularly interested in the conversion of tambu into cash and vice versa. In fact on the Gazelle Peninsula Tolai very rarely sold tambu for cash. Another complicating factor was that they had no standard conversion rate between the number of individual shells and one fathom. There were separate terms for individual numbers of shells, such as two, six, ten, twelve, as well as for a fathom and fractions thereof, but I never met a Tolai who knew how many single shells made up one fathom. My Tolai assistant, to whom I first put the question, was completely perplexed and could not grasp why I wanted this piece of information.

Cash and tambu existed side by side as media of exchange, but whereas cash fulfilled only a purely economic function, tambu also acted as an element in social cohesion. Therefore, though tambu was a highly liquid asset, the people displayed little interest in its liquidity. It was the seller rather than the buyer who decided whether particular transactions were conducted in tambu or cash. I observed on a number of occasions vendors insisting on tambu payment and allowing prospective buyers to pass by rather than accepting cash for their produce. On the other hand, I never saw a market seller refusing to accept tambu payment when it was offered. For instance, a Matupi woman seller of fish when asked how much she thought she would get replied that she was

> selling for *tambu* and did not know how much she would make. In fact she received 10 fathoms. Her brother, with whom I discussed the point, explained that had she sold for cash, she would have received £3 to £4, but added that since his sister wanted tambu she was not primarily concerned about profit (Epstein, A.L., 1963a: 207).

Though only about 10 per cent of total market turnover was settled in tambu (see Table 21), as much as 25 per cent of all intra-Tolai transactions were paid in tambu rather than cash. Vendors carefully collected the small strips of twelve or twenty shells which they received in payment for their sales of areca nut, pepper, lime or peanuts and took them back to their

Table 21

Cash and tambu trade, Rabaul market
(percentages)

Date	Produce brought			Produce sold			Unsold produce		
	Cash	Tambu	Total	Cash	Tambu	Total	Cash	Tambu	Total
Weekdays									
1/6/61	93	7	100	95	5	100	90	10	100
2/6/61	87	13	100	85	15	100	91	9	100
5/6/61	94	6	100	96	4	100	89	11	100
6/6/61	90	10	100	85	15	100	84	16	100
7/6/61	85	15	100	88	12	100	73	27	100
Saturdays									
3/6/61	95	5	100	97	3	100	99	1	100
17/6/61	82	18	100	82	18	100	83	17	100
Weekday average	90	10	100	90	10	100	85	15	100
Saturday average	88	12	100	89	11	100	91	9	100

home parishes, where they laboriously joined all the small pieces and measured their tambu takings in fathoms. Tambu trade persisted because considerable importance was still attached to tambu in social life. For instance, if a woman had a son of marriageable age she was expected to accumulate tambu so as to be able to contribute to his bridewealth. Women vendors in such circumstances were, therefore, prepared to sell for tambu only. On the other hand, if a seller had her eyes on some article, such as clothing, in one of the Rabaul shops, she obviously preferred cash payment for her produce. Accordingly, the price for each item sold both for tambu and cash was fixed by supply and demand operating independently in the tambu and in the cash sectors. During my survey of Rabaul market a chicken could be bought for one fathom tambu or 10/- to 12/- in cash, while six taro cost half a fathom or 2/-. In the one case, one fathom equalled 10/-, in the other it equalled only 4/-. This meant that the cash demand for chickens was greater in relation to its supply than that for taro, while the reverse held true for the tambu sector. Similarly, ten to twelve *malabur* (small sprat-like fish) were sold by Matupi vendors for 1/- or $\frac{1}{4}$ fathom tambu (Epstein, A.L., 1963a: 192), whereas thirty-six areca nuts, three bundles of peanuts or three small bags of lime could be bought for 1/- or thirty-six shells which, according to my count, amounted to only one tenth of a fathom. In spite of the fact that Tolai had the theoretical concept of a uniform exchange rate, in practice tambu prices for food items were not generally equated at a uniform rate with their cash prices.

In theory, this varying exchange rate would appear to give enterprising men the opportunity of manipulating the two sectors of the economy in such a way as to accumulate tambu or cash as they wished. If, for instance, a Tolai wanted to accumulate cash, he might be tempted to convert £1 into £3 by buying taro with cash, selling the taro for tambu, then buying chickens with the tambu and selling them for cash. Similar transactions were in fact made by Rapitok villagers, when they bought coconuts with tambu and sold the copra for cash (see p. 75). If this arbitrage had been done on a large enough scale it would eventually have brought about a uniform exchange rate. However, there were a number of considerations which militated against the actual development of such a practice. There was a large surplus of unsold produce left over at every market day. The weekday average of unsold cash produce was as much as 33 per cent, while the Saturday average was 26 per cent; unsold tambu produce averaged 49 per cent on weekdays, but only 15 per cent on Saturdays (see Table 22). Moreover, the total range of transactions con-

Table 22

Sold and unsold produce, Rabaul market (percentages)

Date	Cash produce			Tambu produce		
	Sold	Unsold	Total	Sold	Unsold	Total
Weekdays						
1/6/61	65	35	100	45	55	100
2/6/61	60	40	100	72	28	100
5/6/61	60	40	100	33	67	100
6/6/61	74	26	100	52	48	100
7/6/61	76	24	100	55	45	100
Saturdays						
3/6/61	77	23	100	96	4	100
17/6/61	72	28	100	74	26	100
Weekday average	67	33	100	51	49	100
Saturday average	74	26	100	85	15	100

ducted in tambu was limited in relation to the total market turnover; tambu transactions formed only 11 per cent of total sales at Rabaul market (see Table 21). Since tambu was restricted to intra-Tolai trade and very few Tolai ever wanted to buy chickens, it was unlikely that sufficient tambu buyers would be interested in purchasing chickens to increase their tambu price and decrease their cash price. Most of the demand for chickens came from the Chinese who had to pay in cash because they had no means of acquiring tambu. Similarly, since the major part of the demand for taro came from the Tolai themselves, who were the only buyers having tambu at their disposal, it was unlikely that many of them would prefer to purchase taro with cash so as to reduce the tambu and increase the cash price. With an ever-declining tambu sector of the economy, it is now unlikely that an equalisation in the exchange rate will ever occur.

In my evaluation of trade transactions in tambu I used an exchange rate of 10/- per fathom. This was based on the fact that by far the majority of tambu sales were in peanuts, areca nuts and lime, for which the purchasing parity of one fathom tambu was 10/-.

No credit sales were ever conducted on the market. Cash or tambu had to be handed over there and then before the vendor was prepared to part with her produce. Native food, like non-indigenous types of goods, was arranged in lots of 1/- or multiples thereof, or in units of shell money. Six dry coconuts or four green coconuts sold for 1/-, while six small taro sold for 2/- and six large taro for 3/- or 4/-, one bundle of peanuts sold for twelve shells, one small packet of lime for twelve shells and a medium packet for twenty shells.

There were some minor price fluctuations from day to day for native produce, due to accidents of varying supply and demand, yet there was very little seasonal variation in native food production, and therefore hardly any seasonal price fluctuations. Altogether, prices of native foods were much less flexible than those of non-indigenous types. However, if on a Saturday there was by chance a short supply of taro while a forthcoming feast in one of the coastal parishes created a big demand, six small taro were sold for 3/- and six large for 4/-, while on other market days, when there was ample supply and comparatively little demand, six small taro sold for 2/- and six large for 3/-. The prices for native foods were only very rarely reduced in the course of a day. Furthermore, goods which varied only little in size, as for instance coconuts, had fixed prices.

Although native food prices were fairly static in the short run, there had been considerable increases, at least in terms of tambu prices, since the turn of the century. Danks reports that in 1887 fifty or sixty taro could be bought with one fathom, while in 1961 only twelve or eighteen were sold for that amount; twelve areca nuts could be bought with four shells in Danks's days (1887: 308), while they cost twelve shells in 1961. Thus tambu prices approximately trebled during the last seventy-five years. However, short-run prices were as stable then as they were in 1961. Danks remarked in 1887 that 'all articles of food remain at much the same price'.

The lack of flexibility in native food prices may be attributed to a number of causes. Firstly, the absence of seasonal variations makes for constant supply and consequently constant supply prices throughout the year. Moreover the widespread network of social relations among the Tolai not only linked sellers with each other but also established social connections between sellers and Tolai buyers; a buyer was often a relative or friend of the vendor. Standard prices eliminated the ill-feeling in personal relations caused by price differences and bargaining between buyer and seller. They also cut out the hazards of competition and price fluctuations.

According to my calculations, only 14 per cent of the turnover on Saturday was accounted for by non-Tolai native buyers, while Tolai purchasers made up as much as 42 per cent. Moreover, it was practically impossible to charge different prices for the same commodities to Tolai and non-Tolai buyers. Therefore, firm prices were the easiest and best means of facilitating trade among natives. However, as most items sold varied in size and quality and goods were neither graded nor sold by weight, buyers still had the option of choosing the size and quality of a particular produce which suited them best.

Furthermore, even if the seller was left with much unsold indigenous types of produce, she could always take it back to her home parish and get her family to consume it, or she may even have been able to sell it to neighbours on the spot. There was little incentive for vendors to reduce prices for native produce in the course of a market day. This was obviously one of the major differences between indigenous and non-indigenous foods. Any unsold non-indigenous food usually represented a complete loss from the point of view of the seller because it was perishable and hardly ever consumed by sellers themselves. By contrast, most native food was not as perishable: lettuces and cabbages were usually dead by the end of the market day, whereas coconuts, areca nuts, yams and sweet potatoes could easily be stored for many weeks without much deterioration; even taro could be stored for a few days at least without coming to any harm.

The Market and the Over-all Tolai Economy

Although the major source of cash income from agricultural produce is derived from the sale of copra and cocoa, Tolai food sales have considerable potential for expansion. The administration and other large institutions, such as mission stations and plantations, frequently placed contracts with individual Tolai suppliers to deliver a certain quantity of sweet potatoes or taro kong kong at weekly or monthly intervals throughout the year at a price fixed in advance. In 1960/1 the rate varied between 1½d. and 2d. per lb. of sweet potatoes or taro kong kong. We have seen that the contractor was usually the owner of a truck (see p. 81), who arranged with relatives or friends from his own and neighbouring parishes to sell to him under his contract, charging them about 35 per cent of the total cash realised for the transport and contract fee. During 1959/60 the administration in Rabaul bought 1,500 tons of truck crops by contract (C.o.A., 1961: 47) and according to my estimate another 1,000 tons were bought under contract from Tolai suppliers by missions and plantations. These 2,500 tons yielded an income of approximately £47,000 which was considerably less than the estimated annual turnover at Rabaul market in 1961 of £130,000 (see Table 23). Thus although large contracts constituted an important part in the sale of food crops, Rabaul market was still by far the major source of income from their sale.

Many individual sellers gathered at Rabaul market, particularly on Saturdays — the average number of vendors who came to the market in June 1961 on weekdays was 150 and on a Saturday 2,112. Each vendor brought only a comparatively small quantity of produce to the market. The average turnover per vendor on a weekday amounted to no more than 14/7 and on a Saturday to £1/15/11 (see Table 24). During the week 33 per cent of all vendors sold produce worth less than 10/- per day and only 2 per cent sold more than £2 worth of produce. Saturday sales were, however, considerably higher; only 16 per cent sold goods for less than 10/- each, whereas as many as 19 per cent sold more than £2 worth. Both for weekdays and Saturdays the modal turnover lay in the range between 10/- and £1 (see Table 25).

Indigenous produce and non-indigenous vegetables constituted the two most important categories of produce entering Rabaul market. On weekdays the former made up 52 per cent and the latter 36 per cent of produce brought to the market; the respective percentages for Saturday were 46 per cent and 40 per cent (see Table 26). On weekdays, however, when fewer native buyers attended the market, as much as 46 per cent of indigenous produce remained unsold, whereas relatively more Europeans and Chinese did their marketing during the week and as much as 79 per cent of non-indigenous vegetables was sold. On Saturdays about one-quarter of indigenous and one-third of non-indigenous produce remained unsold (see Table 27). However, a large part of non-indigenous produce was hawked by vendors round the town after they had been

Table 23

Average value of produce and net income, Rabaul market

Period	Average value of goods sold £	Average net trading income £
Per weekday[a]	110	90
Per Saturday[a]	2,739	2,200
Per week[a]	3,290	2,650
Per month[a]	13,160	10,600
Per 4 months peak trade[a]	52,640	42,400
Per 4 months slack trade[b]	35,110	28,300
Per 4 months interim trade[c]	42,110	33,900
Per year	130,000	105,000
Annual intra-Tolai trade[d]	78,000	—

[a]Figures based on June 1961 survey.
[b]Estimated at two-thirds of peak trade.
[c]Estimated at 80 per cent of peak trade.
[d]I estimate that throughout the whole year 60 per cent of total trade conducted at Rabaul Market was intra-Tolai.

Table 24

Average and total produce, Rabaul market

Date	Number of sellers			Average per seller														Market total		
	Sample	Counted	Estimated upper limit	Produce brought			Produce sold			Produce unsold		Transport charge		Net income			Produce brought nearest	Produce sold nearest	Produce unsold nearest
				£	s.	d.	£	s.	d.	s.	d.	s.	d.	£	s.	d.	£	£	£
Weekdays																			
1/6/61	24	179	196	1	0	0		12	5	7	7	3	3		9	2	196	122	74
2/6/61	29	116	128	1	1	8		13	1	8	7	3	6		9	7	139	84	55
5/6/61	27	91	100	1	1	7		13	0	8	7	3	3		9	10	108	65	43
6/6/61	25	144	160	1	4	2		17	6	6	8	3	6		14	0	193	140	53
7/6/61	32	143	158	1	3	0		16	10	6	2	3	7		13	3	182	132	50
Saturdays																			
3/6/61	76	1,850	2,035	1	9	7	1	3	2	6	5	5	2		18	0	3,010	2,357	653
17/6/61	70	1,990	2,190	1	19	6	1	8	6	11	0	4	7	1	3	11	4,325	3,121	1,204
Weekday average	27	135	150	1	2	1		14	7	7	6	3	5		11	2	164	110	54
Saturday average	73	1,920	2,112	1	14	6	1	5	11	8	8	4	10	1	1	0	3,667	2,739	928

Table 25

Distribution of produce sold per vendor in sample sellers, Rabaul market

	Weekdays										Saturdays				Average			
£	1/6/61		2/6/61		5/6/61		6/6/61		7/6/61		3/6/61		17/6/61		Weekday		Saturday	
	No.	%	No.	%	No.	%	No.	%	No.	%	No.	%	No.	%	No.	%	No.	%
0.00-0.49	8	34	9	31	10	37	8	32	10	32	15	20	8	12	8	33	12	16
0.50-0.99	11	46	13	45	11	41	7	28	11	36	21	29	21	30	11	39	21	30
1.00-1.49	4	16	2	7	5	19	7	28	7	22	15	20	15	21	5	19	15	21
1.50-1.99			4	14	1	3	2	8	3	10	12	15	9	13	2	7	10	14
2.00-2.49	1	4	1	3			1	4			9	11	8	12	1	2	9	11
2.50-2.99											3	4	4	5			3	4
3.00 and over											1	1	5	7			3	4
Total	24	100	29	100	27	100	25	100	32	100	76	100	70	100	27	100	73	100

Table 26

Types of produce entering and sold, Rabaul market
(percentages)

Date	Indigenous crops		Cooked food		Fish and chicken		Fruit and eggs		Non-indigenous vegetables		Total value	
	Brought	Sold	Brought	Sold	Brought	Sold	Brought	Sold	Brought	Sold	Brought	Sold
												£
Weekdays												
1/6/61	57	48	–	–	–	–	6	4	35	48	196	122
2/6/61	55	51	2	3	2	–	4	5	37	41	139	84
5/6/61	55	46	5	8	–	–	7	7	33	39	108	65
6/6/61	46	36	2	3	4	5	2	3	46	50	193	140
7/6/61	45	37	12	12	–	–	14	14	29	37	182	132
Saturdays												
3/6/61	49	51	1	2	2	3	5	6	43	38	3,010	2,359
17/6/61	43	41	8	9	4	6	8	7	37	37	4,325	3,121
Weekday average	52	44	4	7	1	1	7	6	36	42	164	110
Saturday average	46	46	4	5	3	5	7	6	40	38	3,667	2,759

Table 27

Types of sold and unsold produce, Rabaul market (percentages)

Date	Indigenous crops		Cooked food		Fish and chicken		Fruit and eggs		Non-indigenous vegetables	
	Sold	Unsold	Sold	Unsold	Sold	Unsold	Sold	Unsold	Sold	Unsold
Weekdays										
1/6/61	49	51	–	–	–	–	50	50	84	16
2/6/61	51	49	100	–	–	100	83	17	73	27
5/6/61	50	50	100	–	–	–	67	33	70	30
6/6/61	61	39	97	3	100	–	84	16	78	22
7/6/61	59	41	80	20	–	–	73	27	90	10
Saturdays										
3/6/61	83	17	100	–	75	25	92	8	70	30
17/6/61	65	35	76	24	100	–	83	17	68	32
Weekday average	54	46	94	6	50	50	71	29	79	21
Saturday average	74	26	88	12	88	12	88	12	69	31

unsuccessful at the market. All unsold native food was taken back to the parish and consumed there. Each day when the market broke up at about 4 p.m. or 5 p.m., one could see large baskets full of taro, areca nuts and other native foods being loaded on to the trucks which came to take vendors back to their home parishes. This clearly indicates that there was a considerable surplus of native food brought to the market for which some outlet ought to be found.

There are several possibilities of providing an expanding market for native produce: firstly, the administration as well as plantations and mission stations could be encouraged to substitute taro, taro kong kong, and sweet potatoes for rice as part of the rations they issue to their native employees. Secondly, it might be an idea for these institutions to provide their labour force with areca nuts, peppers, and lime instead of the free tobacco issue. This would not only act as a boost to the native economy but also result in a reduction of imports of rice and tobacco, which would be beneficial to the economy of the Territory as a whole. Thirdly, vendors might be encouraged to sell their produce by weight rather than in 1/- lots; this could be done by providing either a large number of small scales or a few large ones at the market. In turn this might help to increase the volume of sales by enabling each buyer to purchase the exact quantity he desired at a certain price per lb. Fourthly, the cooked food sector of the market could quite easily be expanded. None of the cooked food was ever taken back to the home parish by vendors; they consumed part of their own supplies while offering it to prospective buyers. On weekdays when sellers did not stay as long at the market as on Saturdays, they consumed only 6 per cent of their cooked food supplies, whereas on Saturdays, when they remained at the market till late in the afternoon, they ate as much as 12 per cent. Since, as we have seen, visits to the market for sellers as well as for many buyers were largely social ventures and not economic enterprises, there was a considerable demand for cooked food. Thus it should be possible to arrange snack bars at the market, where cooked taro, spinach, tapioca, wild fowl eggs and other foods could be sold. These snack bars could also sell drinks of green coconut juice, as well as *ku,* a coconut relish.

In this way a large part of the native food surplus might be absorbed economically.

On weekdays, vendors normally came only from parishes situated in the immediate vicinity of Rabaul; a number of them simply walked to the market carrying their produce in large bags from a strap hung round their forehead. Consequently the average transport charge per weekday vendor was only 3/5 as compared with 4/11 on Saturdays when vendors came from further afield. On Saturdays transport charges per vendor ranged from 1/- to 12/-, whereas on weekdays the range was from 1/- to 6/- only. The total outlay by sellers on transport charges on a Saturday in June 1961 amounted to approximately £500 of which about 80 per cent was pocketed by Tolai vehicle owners. Income from transport charges was of course considerably higher than £400 on a Saturday, since a great number of men also travelled to Rabaul and paid for their return fares. Thus the market not only enabled Tolai to derive an income from the sale of produce but it also provided further impetus to economic development by creating a substantial demand for regular transport facilities.

On the basis of my survey I attempted to calculate the annual turnover at Rabaul market. Since there was considerable variation in the supply of produce between the flush months from June to September and the slack months from December to March, with October and November, April and May providing transitional periods, I made the very conservative estimate that turnover during the transitional months amounted to only 80 per cent and during the slack months to only 66 per cent of the peak trade I recorded in June.

This is a minimum estimate, because during the slacker months higher prices compensated at least to a certain extent for smaller supplies and the seasonal variation was largely restricted to non-indigenous produce. A 20 per cent reduction in turnover value during the transitional months implies that the quantity of non-indigenous produce was about halved, while a third reduction in value during the slack months amounted to a two-thirds reduction in the quantity of non-indigenous purchases at the market. Rabaul had in 1961 a European and Chinese community of about 4,000. Therefore during the peak months the value of the weekly consumption of market produce per head of non-indigenous population in Rabaul amounted to about 7/-. This compares with a per capita value of consumption by non-indigenes of 3/6 during interim months and of 2/4 during the slack months. If we bear in mind that during slack months prices were higher than during peak months and the quantity of produce 2/4 bought was much less in January than in June, my estimate of annual turnover is seen to be a minimum rather than a maximum.

I also calculated that in 1961 £78,000, or about 60 per cent of the total annual turnover, came from intra-Tolai trade. This calculation is based on the percentage of total purchases in June 1961 made by Tolai at the market — about 40 per cent (see Table 28). My calculation of the proportion of turnover

Table 28

Transactions by different categories of buyers, Rabaul market[a] (percentages)

Date	European	Chinese	Tolai Vendors	Tolai Other	Papuan	New Guinea	Total
Weekdays							
1/6/61	15	38	4	29	8	6	100
2/6/61	20	20	15	28	2	15	100
5/6/61	12	32	7	22	2	25	100
6/6/61	12	41	13	19	2	13	100
7/6/61	15	33	12	24	4	12	100
Saturdays							
3/6/61	23	24	8	28	4	13	100
17/6/61	14	28	11	36	2	9	100
Weekday average	15	33	10	24	4	14	100
Saturday average	18	26	10	32	3	11	100

[a]This table is only an estimate.

accounted for by the different categories of buyers is only a rough approximation, since I did not concern myself at the time of the survey with investigating the demand side of the market. There were some Europeans buying on behalf of indigenes, such as the European buyer for the Nonga native hospital; on the other hand, there were also native domestic servants purchasing for their European or Chinese employers' households. Yet the overall picture emerging from Table 28 is reinforced by my data on the proportion of types of produce sold at Rabaul market (see Table 26), which indicate that slightly less than half the produce (by value) sold in June 1961 was non-indigenous food items. This coincides closely with the percentages of European and Chinese purchases shown in Table 28. This in turn strengthens the basis for my assumption that the figure of 40 per cent Tolai purchases in June 1961 is fairly accurate. Furthermore, in my estimate of annual intra-Tolai transactions I made an allowance for the reduced proportion of non-indigenous purchases during interim and slack months.

Summing up the discussion of Tolai market trading we can say that in spite of the fact that Rabaul market seemed to provide the ideal conditions for the operation of perfect competition, the many individual small vendors faced their buyers as one monopolistic group rather than competing with each other for trade. In the short period, prices of indigenous food items were almost completely stable and fixed in advance; prices for non-indigenous food produce were slightly more flexible. Vendors sold their produce in lots of 1/- and based their decisions as to the size of the individual lot (that is, the prices) on the level of supply; they appeared to assume a constant demand. If in the course of the market day demand did not come up to expectation, sellers tended to reduce prices for non-indigenous produce; they never increased their prices, even in the face of extensive demand. Prices throughout the market were almost uniform. If any vendor intended to reduce prices she consulted her immediate neighbours and only when a group of them agreed did any of them increase the quantity of her 1/- lots. Most sellers of the same commodity then followed suit. Tolai 'primitive affluence', accompanied by a rather narrow cash demand horizon, mitigated against the development of keen competition among vendors. The widespread social network further prevented underbidding by sellers. Moreover, Tolai customary reluctance to show greed prevented vendors from offering their wares beyond passively displaying them to prospective buyers. Social considerations thus impeded the development of professional market traders who, from an economic point of view, would have been much more efficient vendors and would have considerably reduced the cost of trading.

8

Conclusion

In the course of this book I have tried to give an account of the major aspects of Tolai expansion. I discussed the mutual interaction and relationship between the traditional social system and new economic activities; I argued that the customary social system had been so flexible that it managed to survive with only few changes, in spite of radical alterations in economic circumstances. The quite considerable pace of economic growth shows a quick and positive response to the new economic opportunities which were created by European contact. This in turn raises the question of what was the secret of Tolai success? What general lesson in the sphere of economic development can be learned from this case study? In these concluding pages I want first of all to discuss it in a broader theoretical framework and then outline a few of the practical implications which may provide some guidance to the encouragement of cumulative growth in small-scale underdeveloped societies in general.

Theoretical Framework

I have shown that economic development passed through a number of phases since first European contact. It now remains to examine the logical possibility of this providing a schema of growth for other small societies. In order to do this I shall try to separate from each phase those factors which were peculiar to the Tolai case from those which I regard as likely to occur in other instances.

The Tolai were very fortunate in their pre-conditions of growth: their environment provided them with abundant and extremely fertile soils, and they were blessed with an excellent natural harbour in Blanche Bay. Within this favourable environment they had already developed, before European contact, an extensive network of trade facilitated by shell money. Furthermore, their political and social system was highly flexible, allowing for the success of individual enterprise and thrift rather than emphasising ascribed status. These I regard as the factors peculiar to Tolai economic development, in particular the first phase. In all instances of first contact, links are established with the wider cash economy. These may consist of the sale of agricultural produce or migration of labour to places of work. Evidence from the Tolai, as well as from other culture areas, indicates that in the early stages of growth an indigenous population, if given the choice, will prefer to sell produce rather than labour.* This reaction appears to continue until urban centres in the area progress so far as to offer great attractions such as cinemas, restaurants, coffee shops and beer halls not available in the rural hinterland. However, immediately after first contact indigenous people appear to prefer to remain in their customary settlements rather than venture as migrant labourers, provided they are able to participate in the wider economy by selling their produce. This attitude helps to provide at least some element of social continuity even under changing conditions.

If a people is contacted for the first time and wishes to sell agricultural produce for cash, but is not accustomed to producing a surplus, it must either reduce its subsistence consumption or invest labour in the extension of cultivation. During the first contact period, there is likely to be a reduction of subsistence consumption or a reduction of waste or both. The length of this 'transition period' will depend largely on the attraction of the new goods offered to the natives, their entrepreneurial qualities, their personal contact with expatriate business activities and the effective pacification of the area. In some cases the 'transition period' may last only a few years. In the Tolai case the period lasted about twenty-five years, because the

* However, very often through poor communication and long distances, the opportunity for such choice in real terms does not come until a later stage of development.

people were at first still keen on accumulating shell money rather than acquiring the goods offered them by traders. Moreover, the majority of men were reluctant to take up employment with Europeans and therefore few of them had first-hand experience of European enterprise. Those who were prepared to work for expatriates, and whom I called migrants, in fact became innovators in their home parishes on their return from their spell of employment. They were the first to start cash cropping. Many villagers followed the example set them by migrants.

The passing from the 'transition' to the 'agricultural investment period' is marked by a rapid expansion of cash crops. If this involves new and unknown produce as well as novel methods of cultivation it can succeed only if there are in existence competent organs of public administration (Galbraith, 1965: 42). On the other hand, provided sales are made up of traditional crops cash output can easily be superimposed on subsistence farming. In this case the customary economic and social organisation may be re-affirmed.

The establishment of new perennial tree gardens fits naturally into the traditional methods of shifting cultivation, both food crops and trees being planted on the newly cleared land. Several crops of food can be taken off the land, which is then given up entirely to trees (Hills, 1956: 106). As long as the cash produce requires little labour and the other factors of production required are in ample supply this will further help to perpetuate the traditional social system. The emphasis, at least at first, will be on continuity rather than change. Since the expansion of cash cropping in underdeveloped societies usually involves mainly an increased labour input without much application of capital, increased consumption is normally a concomitant of increased agricultural capital formation. As long as population pressure on land resources does not cause low returns per unit of labour, consumption and investment are complementary; the higher level of consumption induces additional and more productive effort, which serves to generate incomes which in turn render possible increased consumption and encourage further capital formation (Bauer and Yamey, 1957: 140). It is during this period that natives first become aware of time as an element in the production process, and the first clocks and watches appear in their homes.

During the first half of the 'agricultural investment period' the Tolai's increased consumption was accompanied by extensive cash crop cultivation. The increased consumption during the second half of the period was sustained by increased income resulting from both higher copra prices and an increased copra output from previous plantings. This decreased rate of agricultural capital formation was a direct result of the economic stagnation in the whole New Guinea economy in the 1920s. Therefore, in other small-scale societies there is likely to be a steady increase in the rate of agricultural capital formation. Wherever the traditional social system manages to survive largely unchanged after the first impact of European contact, we can expect a decreasing marginal propensity to consume soon after the most urgent cash requirements of new tools and clothing have been satisfied. Under such conditions cash purchases will be regarded as not really essential and therefore will show a high elasticity of demand.

The length of the 'agricultural investment period' depends on how long it takes the particular cash crop to mature, the rate of population and income growth, the intensity of consumers' demand, the degree of contact with expatriate enterprise, investment opportunities, and whether or not the traditional economic organisation provided for joint ownership of assets. If the cash crop matures quickly and income grows at a rapid rate, say because of rising prices of exports, while population increases only slowly, the marginal propensity to consume soon begins to fall and there are migrants who are aware of attractive investment opportunities coupled with a traditional system of corporate ownership, the period will be very short, otherwise it may be quite extended.

In any case, the accumulation of considerable cash reserves, fortified by an increasing marginal propensity to save, together with the experience of European ventures, will lead some natives sooner or later to start investing in productive assets outside agriculture. The first attempts at such investment, usually made by migrants, mark the transition from the 'agricultural investment' to the 'investment trial period'. In societies such as the Tolai, who derive most of their cash income from the sale of agricultural produce, the first investment efforts will most likely occur in the agricultural processing or service industries in general; for example the establishment of copra driers or cocoa fermentaries or retail or transport facilities. However, in view of the low level of general education and the lack of managerial and accountancy training among peoples of underdeveloped areas, there are bound to be a large number of failures among the first ventures. Although initially a system of group ownership assists capital formation by offering larger funds for investment through the pooling of resources by a whole group of individuals, the economic flexibility and mobility required during this period of 'investment trials' will eventually undermine the traditional system of corporate ownership of assets. Consequently, we may expect the first political rebellion during this period, such as the Young Men's *Kiwungs* among the Tolai. It is during this period that economic planners and administrative officials in general can offer the greatest assistance to economic development by providing advice to natives on the formation of joint stock companies or co-operatives, by giving them managerial training, offering accountancy services and so on. The length of the 'investment trial period' will largely depend on the speed with which natives acquire the necessary managerial skills to run successful enterprises and the state of the world market. Among the Tolai, the 'investment trial period' was interrupted by the war and Japanese occupation, and its end was hastened after the war by very favourable prices of exports on the world market.

After years of experimenting with investment, the time should come when the majority of ventures becomes successful. This marks the transition from the 'investment trial' to the 'tertiary investment period'. In view of the small size of the home market and the lack of knowledge of world markets, the most successful ventures by natives are likely to be the provision of tertiary services such as transport and retail trading. This industry, by its very nature, is protected from foreign though not from expatriate competition. Ready advice to native entrepreneurs on the prospects of investment in manufacturing industries, as well as the necessary training in mechanical and managerial skills, may help to redirect investment from tertiary to secondary industries. However, the small size of the home market hampers the establishment of firms producing import substitutes and inexperience prevents attempts to compete in export markets of manufacturing produce. The Ghana migrant cocoa farmers invested their profits from cocoa farming in processing equipment and lorries (Hill, 1963: 191). 'In the typical African or Asian economy, agriculture produces something like 50 per cent of gross domestic product, services account for 35 per cent and industry for only 15 per cent' (Lewis, 1966: 154).

The economic relationship of small-scale expanding economies with the rest of the world will invariably be one whereby crops such as cocoa, coffee, copra or cotton will be exported and manufactured articles, as well as some food not available locally, will be imported. Unless many different crops are exported the economy will be extremely vulnerable to price fluctuations on the world market. Yet as long as ample land is available and cash crops have a low labour input, we can expect the indigenous supply to have a low elasticity. Therefore, tertiary investment will be accompanied by a steady rate of expansion of cash crops until the supply of land becomes exhausted. As soon as land becomes a scarce resource the disadvantages of the lack of economic diversification will present a crucial problem. Unless world prices for primary produce rise, the rate of expansion is bound to slow down drastically or even come to a halt altogether. However, since the prospects of developing manufacturing industries on any scale are poor in newly growing small economies, unless based on mineral deposits, a diversification of cash crops accompanied by efficient servicing and processing facilities is essential. 'A sensible community should fight against over-specialization. Money must be spent on research, training and investment in commodities, which are not now as profitable or do not now seem as promising as the dominant export' (Lewis, 1966: 42).

In the particular case of the Territory of Papua and New Guinea, the contribution to world trade of any of its export crops is far too small to allow any influence over prices. In order to protect small underdeveloped countries against the adverse effects of price fluctuations in the world market on their balance of payments, it is advisable for them to diversify their exports as much as is economically feasible.

A growing cash sector must be expected to have its repercussions in the social and political sphere too. The rate of social change will be inversely related to the ease with which new cash earning activities can be combined with the traditional way of life. The low labour input of Tolai subsistence and cash crops facilitated a high degree of continuity in social institutions. This emerges clearly from an examination of their economic and social differentiation. Only those few Rapitok migrants who came to occupy the position of matrilineage section elder managed to acquire a considerable amount of productive assets. The traditional social differentiation between elders, middle-farmers and single men re-asserted itself under the new economic activities and is still much more pronounced than the new differentiation between migrants and villagers. It would be interesting to compare and contrast the continuity in Tolai social life with the change in similar societies, where the newly introduced cash crops required so much labour that they could not easily be combined with the customary way of life. To my knowledge no such studies are as yet available. In the Tolai case the importance of subsistence fish and food crops provides for the continued use of tambu as indigenous currency. Tambu in turn acts as backbone to the traditional social organisation. Thus a high degree of self-sufficiency in food, that is, a reasonably large and constant subsistence sector, can be expected to help perpetuate the customary way of life. This is likely to delay, and may even prevent, the development of professional middlemen in the marketing of produce, as in the Tolai case. This may then result in monopolistic market pricing tendencies in spite of otherwise ideal conditions for the operation of perfect competition — large numbers of small sellers and buyers and a general knowledge of quality and prices of produce.

In societies with systems of matrilineal descent and inheritance accompanied by patri-virilocal residence we can expect growing tensions in social relations as soon as perennial cash crops and costly indivisible assets appear on the scene. 'It is because all these new activities are not independent of the existing institutions into which they have to be fitted, and which have in turn to be adjusted to them, that the process of change is so complex and — if it is to proceed harmoniously — necessarily so slow' (Frankel, 1953: 24). The more flexible the conditions, the smoother the process of development. 'If the area of cocoa-farming land (purchased and available) increases as rapidly as the number of cocoa-farming members of the appropriate matrilineage, then there may be no reason why a conflict should develop' (Hill, 1963: 127). By contrast with the Tolai, the Aburi migrant cocoa farmer of south Ghana was able to relieve tensions within his matrilineage by either buying land for his sons or associating with his wife's brother in purchasing land which eventually would come under his sons' control. It was as unlikely that an Aburi matrilineage would give one of its members permission to grant portions of its own land to his sons as it was that he would ever apply for such permission — the remedy for this was in his own hands, namely the purchase of other land (Hill, 1963: 129).

The Aburi operated in a frontier context: they still had the opportunity of acquiring as much cocoa land as they wished. This may account for the fact that Aburi farmers successfully adhered to their traditional system of matrilineage inheritance when they migrated and bought 'family lands'. Judging from the Tolai case study, it is likely that the Aburi will experience difficulties in their social organisation as soon as population begins to press on land resources. The foregoing chapters certainly exemplify the adverse effects of matrilineal inheritance of corporately owned land on economic expansion as soon as shortage of land occurs.

The Tolai system of inheritance prevents them from giving their own cocoa project full support and consequently slows down the rate of economic expansion. Moreover, it leads to quarrels and disputes between individuals and often even between whole groups. These tensions are heightened by the onset of land shortages, which will in turn undermine the influence of traditional kin-groups. Altogether, the decline of the importance of large kin-groups accompanied by a growing emphasis on the nuclear family appears to be a frequent concomitant of economic growth (Bailey, 1957: 92).

This process is normally associated with a change of control over assets; property vested in a large kin-group is divided into parcels of individual property. Since political authority is usually closely associated with control over resources, a change in the system of ownership and inheritance is bound to effect a change in political institutions too. It seems that in order to facilitate industrial expansion the formation of centralised political administration becomes essential. For instance, the Tolai Cocoa Project could be started only after the formation of native local government councils in the area. A centralised political administration also enables entrepreneurs to draw on funds from a larger number of people. It helps to de-centralise ownership of productive assets while at the same time centralising the administration of enterprises. Political centralisation may be the result of indigenous strife or be superimposed by the colonial administration; whichever it be, it sets the stage for further, more rapid economic growth.

As we have seen, the rate of social change in small-scale societies may be very slow for some time after first contact with the world economy. There may be stress on social continuity rather than change. However, as soon as the economy approaches a critical stage, as when the supply of land is beginning to be exhausted and radical changes in the system of land ownership and inheritance become vital for continued expansion, we must expect social change to become more rapid and at the same time more revolutionary.

The schema of economic growth of small underdeveloped societies, as it emerged from the Tolai case study, appears, when abstracted from its specific background, to be logically likely to fit other similar societies in Melanesia and elsewhere. However, the efficacy of the schema will have to be tested by many studies of European contact and the resulting economic and social changes in small societies.

Practical Implications

The initial approach of economists, in the surge of interest after World War II in the problems of growth of low income economies, was to assume that any barriers to growth that

> might exist are economic ones, and that the process of economic growth is adequately dealt with by economic analysis alone (Hagen, 1962: 36).

However, as I have shown, other variables also affect the process of development. The Tolai case study illustrates the crucial part foreign contact — in particular a foreign administration — plays in the sphere of economic development of small-scale societies. Even with such favourable pre-conditions of growth as were found among the Tolai, their economy remained stagnant until its growth potential was fertilised by European contact. Though the people were quick to respond to new economic opportunities, they did not have the inventiveness to start new enterprises of their own accord. The shape and form of their development is entirely due to stimulus originating from outside rather than to spontaneous indigenous ventures. At first the German and subsequently the Australian administration encouraged coconut planting. This ultimately resulted in extensive Tolai copra production. The Japanese ordered rice cultivation, therefore rice was grown. Then, immediately after World War II, the occupation armies offered vehicles cheaply and the Tolai bought them. Since the last war the Australian authorities in the area have sponsored the production of cocoa. Again people followed the lead. The administration thus directly affects the pattern of indigenous economic growth, apart from affecting it indirectly by providing education and other facilities. It is therefore the responsibility of the administration in underdeveloped societies to direct development in the way most beneficial to the indigenous population. In doing this officials may be well advised to bear certain considerations in mind.

The supply of newly introduced cash crops is likely to be fairly inelastic, provided there is still ample land and not much labour is required. This enables marketing boards, set up by the administration, to build up reserve funds by acting as intermediary between indigenous producers and export markets, as long as world market prices for the cash crop are reasonably high. However, here it is important to remember that extension of perennial cash crops can quickly absorb even what used to be an abundant supply of land. I have documented this with reference to Rapitok (see p. 111). As soon as the margin of available cultivable land is approached, with land becoming a scarce resource, the elasticity of the cash crop supply is likely to increase. For instance, a slight fall in cocoa prices might then induce growers to neglect their cocoa trees, or even to chop some down in order to make room for some more remunerative crop or necessary subsistence cultivation. Since perennial cash crops usually involve long-term investment of land and labour, such changing of crops may prove to be disastrous for the total economy. It is important that the indigenous population should be encouraged to diversify their crops as much as is feasible without making cultivation uneconomic. Moreover, it appears advisable to try for some one-season cash produce rather than to depend solely on perennial trees. Although one-season crops are normally more labour intensive than perennial trees, they do have the advantage of quicker returns as well as offering greater flexibility in cultivation.

In societies with 'primitive affluence' and a stress on continuity in social life we can expect a decreasing marginal propensity to consume after an initial expenditure spree, which will result in a growing volume of savings as cash income continues to increase. Consequently, there will be considerable funds lying idle, cash being hoarded awaiting profitable investment. These funds represent an important and valuable opportunity for further development.

> It was the low income elasticity of demand for food, as income increased, which enabled Japan to divert labour to industry, and import equipment, to so great an extent (Clark and Haswell, 1964: 180).

Under such conditions any rise in food prices can be expected to have a more than proportionate negative effect on the volume purchased. To reduce the demand for food imports it may be advisable to introduce some form of purchase or sales tax on rice and tinned fish and meat. The resulting higher prices in turn are likely to encourage the growing of rice and the canning of fish and meat, thereby substituting home production for a considerable volume of imports and relieving balance of payment problems. Plantation interests and overall economic factors would have to be taken into consideration.

However, the conditions of affluence and boom in small underdeveloped societies, resulting from the initial incorporation in the world economy through cash cropping, will soon become jeopardised by population increase accompanied by expansion of cash cropping. In fact the honeymoon with cash cropping draws to a close as soon as shortages of land become apparent. The struggle for land is then likely to undermine the traditional social system, in particular it will affect corporate control over property, which is fairly common in underdeveloped societies. This in turn is bound to lead to strains and stresses within native society. If the rate of economic growth should then decline and stagnation set in, the administration is likely to be blamed for this; intra-indigene hostilities may then be diverted into hostilities against the government, and be responsible for serious upheavals. Economic development provides a challenge to the administration of small-scale underdeveloped societies, which, unless met, may result in serious political disorder.

Bibliography

OFFICIAL PUBLICATIONS

Amtsblatt (1909-1914). *Amtsblatt für das Schutzgebiet Deutsch Neu Guinea.*

B.M.O.G.N.G. (1917). British Military Occupation of German New Guinea, *Government Gazette,* 15 Apr. 1917.

C.o.A. (1914-40). *Administration of the Territory of New Guinea, Annual Reports to the League of Nations.*

——— (1946-65). *Administration of the Territory of New Guinea, Annual Reports to the General Assembly of the United Nations.*

Commonwealth Trade, Customs and Excise Revenue (1913).

Department of the Administrator (1965). Tolai Cocoa Project (mimeograph).

Deutsche Regierung (1911). *Jahresbericht.*

Geographical Handbook Series (1945). *Pacific Islands,* Vol. 5, Naval Intelligence Division.

Nachrichten über Kaiser Wilhelmsland und den Bismarck Archipel (1888).

——— (1891).

——— (1894).

——— (1897).

Neu Guinea Kompagnie (1887). *Geschäftsbericht der Direktion.*

N.B.D.A.E. (1960). New Britain District Agricultural Extension, *Annual Report,* 1959/60.

New South Wales State Register (1884).

(1892). Census and Statistics.

(1896).

Official Handbook (1943). *Official Handbook of the Territory of New Guinea,* Canberra, Government Printer.

Project News Sheet (1960). No. 11.

T.P.N.G. (1952). Territory of Papua and New Guinea, Cocoa Ordinance No. 113.

OTHER REFERENCES

Andrews, J. (1957). 'Land Forms of New Britain', *Australian Geographer,* Vol. 7, No. 1.

Bailey, F.G. (1957). *Caste and the Economic Frontier,* Manchester, Manchester University Press.

Bauer, P.T. and Yamey, B.S. (1957). *The Economics of Underdeveloped Countries,* Cambridge, Cambridge University Press.

Blum, H. (1900). *Neu Guinea und der Bismarck Archipel,* Berlin, Schönfeld and Co.

Braak, C. (1931). 'Klimakunde von Hinterindien und Insulinde' in *Handbuch der Klimatalogie,* Vol. 4/R, Berlin.

Brown, G. (1908). *An Autobiography,* London, Hodder and Stoughton.

Burger, F. (1923). *Unter den Kannibalen der Südsee,* Dresden, Verlag Deutsche Buchwerkstätten.

Clark, C. and Haswell, M. (1964). *The Economics of Subsistence Agriculture,* London, Macmillan and Co. Ltd.

Codere, H. (1950). *Fighting with Property,* New York, Monograph of the American Ethnological Society, Vol. 18.

Crowther, G. (1949). *An Outline of Money,* London, Thomas Nelson and Sons Ltd.

Danks, B. (1887). 'On the Shell Money of New Britain', *Journal of the Royal Anthropological Institute,* Vol. 17.

Einzig, P. (1949). *Primitive Money in its Ethnological, Historical and Economic Aspects,* London, Eyre and Spottiswoode.

Engels, F. (1946). *The Origin of the Family,* London, Lawrence and Wishart Ltd.

Epstein, A.L. (1963a). 'The Economy of Modern Matupit: Continuity and Change on the Gazelle Peninsula', *Oceania,* Vol. 33.

——— (1963b). 'Tambu, a Primitive Shell Money', *Discovery,* December 1963.

——— (1967). 'Urbanization and Social Change in Africa', *Current Anthropology,* Vol. 8, No. 4.

——— and Epstein, T.S. (1962). 'A Note on Population in Two Tolai Settlements', *Journal of the Polynesian Society,* Vol. 71, No. 1.

Epstein, T.S. (1962). *Economic Development and Social Change in South India,* Manchester, Manchester University Press.

——— (1964). 'Personal Capital Formation among the Tolai of New Britain', in Firth, R. and Yamey, B.S. (eds.), *Capital, Saving and Credit in Peasant Societies,* London, George Allen and Unwin Ltd.

Firth, R. (1961). 'Primitive Currency', *Encyclopaedia Britannica,* Vol. 6.

Fisk, E.K. (1962). 'Planning in a Primitive Economy: Special

Problems of Papua and New Guinea', *Economic Record,* Vol. 38.

——— (1964). 'Planning in a Primitive Economy: From Pure Subsistence to the Production of a Market Surplus', *Economic Record,* Vol. 40.

——— (1966). 'The Economic Structure', in Fisk, E.K. (ed.), *New Guinea on the Threshold,* Canberra, Australian National University Press.

Frankel, S.H. (1953). *The Economic Impact on Under-developed Societies,* Oxford, Basil Blackwell.

Galbraith, J.K. (1965). *Economic Development,* Cambridge, Harvard University Press.

Hagen, E.E. (1962). *On the Theory of Social Change,* Homewood (Ill.), The Dorsey Press Inc.

Hahl, A. (1897). 'Über die Rechtsanschauungen der Eingeborenen eines Teiles der Blanchbucht und des Innern der Gazelle Halbinsel', *Nachrichten über Kaiser Wilhelmsland und den Bismarck Archipel.*

Henderson, F.C. (1954). 'Cocoa as a Crop for the Owner-Manager in Papua and New Guinea', *Papua and New Guinea Agricultural Journal,* Vol. 9, No. 2.

Hill, P. (1956). *The Gold Coast Cocoa Farmers,* London, Oxford University Press.

——— (1963). *The Migrant Cocoa-Farmers of Southern Ghana,* Cambridge, Cambridge University Press.

Hogbin, I. and Wedgwood, C. (1953). 'Local Grouping in Melanesia', *Oceania,* Vol. 23.

Keynes, J.M. (1933). *Essays in Persuasion,* London, Macmillan and Co. Ltd.

Kleintitschen, P.A. (1906). *Die Küstenbewohner der Gazelle Halbinsel,* Hiltrop bei Münster, Herz Jesu Missionhaus.

Leahy, M. and Crain, M. (1937). *The Land that Time Forgot,* New York, Funk and Wagnalls Co.

Lewis, W.A. (1966). *Development Planning,* London, George Allen and Unwin Ltd.

Mackenzie, S.S. (1939). *The Australians at Rabaul,* Sydney, Angus and Robertson.

Malinowski, B. (1921). 'The Primitive Economics of the Trobriand Islanders', *Economic Journal,* Vol. 31.

Meek, C.K., MacMillan, W.M., and Hussey, E.R.J. (1940). *Europe and West Africa,* Oxford, Oxford University Press.

Nurkse, R. (1962). *Problems of Capital Formation in Underdeveloped Countries,* Oxford, Basil Blackwell.

Parkinson, R. (1887). *Im Bismarck Archipel: Erlebnisse und Beobachtungen auf der Insel Neu-Pommern (Neu Britanien),* Leipzig, F.A. Brockhaus.

——— (1907). *Dreissig Jahre in der Südsee,* Stuttgart, Verlag von Strecken und Schröder.

Pfeil, J.G. (1899). *Studien und Beobachtungen aus der Südsee,* Braunschweig, Druck und Verlag von Friedrich Viewieg und Sohn.

Pospisil, L. (1963). *Kapauku Papuan Economy,* Yale University Publications in Anthropology, No. 67.

Powell, W. (1883). *Wanderings in a Wild Country,* London, Sampson Low, Marston, Searle and Rivington.

Pullen-Burry, B. (1909). *In a German Colony,* London, Methuen and Co.

Rabaul Times, 18 June 1926.

Rhodes, R.M. (1950). 'Even Prices at the Bung are going Up and Up', *Pacific Islands Monthly,* Vol. 21, No. 3.

Richards, A. (1955). *Practical Planting,* T.P.N.G.

Robson, R.W. (1961). *Handbook of Papua and New Guinea,* Sydney, Pacific Publications Ltd.

Romily, H.H. (1887). 'The Islands of the New Britain Group', *Proceedings of the Royal Geographical Society,* Vol. 9.

Rowley, C.D. (1958). *The Australians in German New Guinea 1914-1921,* Melbourne, Melbourne University Press.

Scharmach, L. (1960). *This Crowd Beats Us All,* Surry Hills, The Catholic Press Newspaper Co. Ltd.

Schnee, H. (1904). *Bilder aus der Südsee,* Berlin, Dietrich Reiner.

Schneider, O. (1905). *Muschelgeldstudien,* Dresden, Verein für Erdkunde.

Shand, R.T. (1966). 'Trade Prospects for the Rural Sector', in Fisk, E.K. (ed.), *New Guinea on the Threshold,* Canberra, Australian National University Press.

South Pacific Post, 8 July 1960.

Williamson, K.R. (1958). 'The Tolai Cocoa Project', *South Pacific,* Vol. 9, No. 13.

Index

For Product Safety Concerns and Information please contact our EU representative GPSR@taylorandfrancis.com
Taylor & Francis Verlag GmbH, Kaufingerstraße 24, 80331 München, Germany

www.ingramcontent.com/pod-product-compliance
Ingram Content Group UK Ltd.
Pitfield, Milton Keynes, MK11 3LW, UK
UKHW022110190926
475702UK00013B/1359
* 9 7 8 1 1 3 8 5 0 7 8 9 0 *